DOPAMINE HOME

RACHEL VERNEY

DOPAMINE HOME

A bold guide to mood-boosting interiors

greenfinch

INTRODUCTION

06	My Story
12	What is Dopamine Decor?
16	The Psychology of Dopamine Decor
20	Find Your Tribe: Types of Dopamine Decor
34	Shoestring Decor

PART ONE:
The Core Principles of Dopamine Decor

42	Bold, Brave Colours
66	Make Mine a Moodboard
70	Colour Palettes
78	The Magic of Paint
84	Get Touchy-feely
88	Embrace Pattern
94	Bring the Outside In
100	Keep It Clean
106	Get the Light Right
112	Plan, Plan, Plan

PART TWO:

The Dopamine Home, Room by Room

118   Living Room
134   Kitchen
148   Dining Room
160   Hallway
170   Bathroom
182   Bedrooms
194   Kids' Rooms
200   Study or Workspace
206   Garden

218   Acknowledgements
220   Resources
221   Picture Credits
222   Index

CONTENTS

My Story

I've always loved bold colours, clashing patterns and beautiful design, but other than a shocking pink bedroom as a teenager, it never really manifested itself in my decor.

For me it was all about clothes, I was fashion girly through and through. I loved how transformative fashion could be, how amazing a new outfit could make you feel, and I wanted to be a part of that process. So, I headed off to London College of Fashion to study as soon as I finished school. It turns out, as much as I loved fashion, I loved partying more. All my artistic intentions fell by the wayside and, before I knew what had happened, I was settled into an office job with a series of uninspired, undecorated rented flats.

In fact, I didn't get the DIY bug until 2020. By then, life had changed dramatically. I was no longer renting; I had bought my first home in Surrey eighteen months before with my partner Jon and our sons Rudi and Arlo. The events that led us to our new home are ones that are still difficult to recall. We had welcomed beautiful twin boys into our family of three in 2017, but just eight weeks later, Kit tragically passed away. I couldn't bear to stay in the London flat where we had lived as it felt empty and incomplete without Kit. From the kitchen where I had made their bottles to the boys' bedroom, I couldn't escape the overwhelming and crushing sadness.

I know there are those grieving who find comfort in being close to where memories have been made, but for us it was the opposite. All we felt was a constant reminder of the life we should have been living.

Thankfully, with the help of our amazing families, we managed to buy an ex-council house in a new area. We were so desperate to move that we didn't even view the property before we bought it. We were on holiday at the time of the open day, so sent Jon's dad and brother to take a look and, based purely on their feedback, we submitted an offer. The first time we stepped inside the front door, we already owned the house — something that seems madness in retrospect but felt right at the time.

The plan was to try and move forwards and heal. Life had other plans, and in 2019 I was diagnosed with cancer. I was thirty-six years old and terrified that I would die, leaving two children under five behind.

Thankfully, my treatment was successful and, just as I was once again ready to try and move forwards, life ground to a halt with the arrival of 2020 and the pandemic. To say I struggled is an understatement; suddenly there were no distractions from the grief and worry of the previous few years. Like so many of us, I felt trapped at home under lockdown and was on the edge of overwhelm. I can't even remember what made me start my first upcycling project now, but I remember the paint colour 'Flamboyant Flamingo' leaping out at me from the Valspar paint chips — a gorgeous rich and vivid coral that just made you smile. I didn't realize it at the time, but I had just discovered the power of dopamine decor.

Starting From Scratch

Our new house was very much a project, it hadn't been updated since the 1980s and was a sea of brown, with the odd pop of shiny green or pink bathroom paint...and not contained to the bathroom! We had assumed it was mostly cosmetic work that needed to be done and planned our renovation budget accordingly, but within the first month we discovered that the whole house needed rewiring, which of course ate up nearly all our savings. We were so busy — first with the small kids and then with me being sick — that we lived with a mish-mash of brown spaces and an occasional half-hearted attempt to cover them up with white paint, for over two years. Eventually, as life started to calm down and we accepted there was no magical windfall about to appear, we had no choice but to have a go and get stuck in with DIY. Luckily, Jon is very handy and, with the help of his family, we began stripping off layers upon layers of paint and wallpaper. And with each layer my confidence grew — it couldn't really look any worse, after all!

From beige and dull, to colourful and fun, my dopamine journey.

My Story

While I was busy decorating and upcycling, one of my best friends suggested I start an Instagram account. She said that while everyone was under house arrest, interior accounts were booming. So, at the time feeling very silly, I posted my very first 'shelfie' and @the_shoestring_home was born. Since then, I've been lucky enough to grow an incredible community of interior fanatics who love dopamine decor just as much as I do and are following me along as I add some joy to our formerly brown house. I wanted people to recognize that if someone like me, who had never done a single DIY project until my late thirties, could do it, then so could they! I would be so happy if, through my Instagram and with this book, I can help more people to unlock the confidence to experiment with colour and design, and to feel brave enough to step outside their comfort zone to create a dream home they didn't think they were capable of.

Your Dopamine Journey...

One of the questions I get asked most frequently about decorating is: where to start? This guide will show you how to begin the journey — whether you're looking for small tweaks with maximum impact to upgrade your space, or whether you're about to embark on a large-scale renovation project. This book will show you how to achieve a joyful, mood-boosting home using simple tips, tricks and creative hacks. Taking you room by room, I will show how to tap into the transformative power of dopamine decor, making your home a happier place to be. This guide will give you the tools and advice you need to embrace the core principle of dopamine decor by inviting bold colours, textures and patterns into your home to curate a space that truly makes you smile. Best of all, in true shoestring form, this book will provide cost-friendly ideas and inspiration for any budget, because I'm a firm believer upgrading your home shouldn't cost you the earth.

...Starts Here

I hope that when you reach the last page, you will be coming away feeling inspired and armed with ideas and tools to start or develop your *Dopamine Home* journey.

I want you to feel empowered to begin applying some of the concepts discussed throughout, to abandon any pre-conditioned design rules you may have been holding onto, and to simply follow your heart to create a home that makes you truly happy. My single most important piece of advice would be: never be afraid of trying something new.

Mistakes can always be undone, but not to ever try, and to potentially miss unlocking something that would make your heart sing, is such a shame.

Enjoy every second of pouring your personality into your home. Having a place that you can call your own, which is a sanctuary where you are safe, content and surrounded by joy, is precious, and so rewarding. Creating your dopamine home is, in all honesty, a labour of love, and this is a journey you will never regret embarking on.

The Flamboyant Flamingo cabinet — the moment I discovered dopamine decor!

My Story

What is Dopamine Decor?

Everything about dopamine decor should spark pleasure.

Dopamine decor is a fairly new trend, but truthfully, it's been around a long time as, put simply, it is the concept of surrounding yourself with decor that brings you joy. Recently, it's picked up this snappy label 'dopamine decor', an offshoot of 'dopamine dressing' as coined by fashion psychologist Dawnn Karen.

Forbes Home describes dopamine decor as 'outfitting your home in colour, textures and patterns that bring you joy...Instead of a specific design aesthetic, it's more about what makes you happy as an individual.' No two dopamine homes are the same, as it's intrinsically linked with *your* personal style and what gets *your* neurotransmitters pumping. Typically, though, dopamine decor is seen as a bold use of colour, energetic patterns, a mixture of textures and an eye for details. This mood-enhancing aesthetic focuses on filling your home with things you love and that make you smile.

For me, my personal dopamine decor is ever evolving as my tastes change, I've always loved bright colours, but now I'm more in tune with the particular tones that bring me joy. I like to be surrounded by energizing and optimistic colours such as oranges, corals and pinks, as well as jewel-toned greens. Botanicals are a recurring theme throughout my home, be they on textiles, wallpapers or in art, as floral and botanical patterns give me pleasure and lift my spirits. Just as I have learned to hone in and identify what boosts my mood and wellbeing, you can too by identifying when and where you feel happiest, and if there are elements of those surroundings that you can incorporate into your own home.

Maximalism

Minimalist interiors have ruled the roost for the past ten years but, as seen in the rise of dopamine decor, there is a shift towards trends that have a more maximalist aesthetic. True maximalism embraces the layering of patterns, textures and colours, typically in a slightly more glamorous way than the playful maximalism of dopamine decor. Maximalist interiors embody 'more is more' – but that doesn't mean just collecting up a load of things you like, chucking them into a room and hoping for the best. Maximalism is still perfectly curated, you just go full volume with the look.

What is Dopamine Decor? ◆ 15

The Psychology of Dopamine Decor

Dopamine is the feel-good hormone that influences a range of our moods and behaviours.

It helps us to feel pleasure, assists motivation and improves our concentration. The link between our neurological response to an interior is central to the psychology of dopamine decor. Designer Joshua Smith puts it beautifully when he says: 'Our perception of beauty and how we incorporate that into our homes can really have a transformative effect on our mental, emotional, and spiritual wellbeing. We're creating a conscious effect where we walk in the door, take in the beauty of our home, and let out an exhale of release. That sigh is the nervous system calming itself down as your brain produces those feel-good hormones thanks to the perceived beauty.'

Making design choices with an emphasis on how they make you feel is fundamental to creating a dopamine home. Colour theory and colour psychology are central principles of dopamine decor (see pages 42–65), as is the use of pattern, nature and texture therapy (see pages 84–99).

An Age-old Wisdom

Though scientific interest and research into the links between interior design and wellbeing have gained momentum in the last decade or so, this isn't a new way of thinking. Theories such as the Indian Vastu Shastra and the Chinese Feng Shui have existed for thousands of years, providing detailed guidelines for how to create a happy home. Now, with the rise of neuroscience, we are more aware than ever before of the importance of our surroundings to our mental health and wellbeing. In recent years, findings of studies have been put to use in hospitals, schools and care homes, to create calming and positive environments for patients, pupils and residents.

People might think that the colour you paint your walls is superficial, but when we are spending so much of our free time in our homes, our decor becomes intricately linked with our mood and happiness. We want our homes to be safe havens where we can feel content.

It's All About You

By learning to tune into your response to your surroundings, being aware of the effects of different visual stimuli, and then using this as a basis to curate your dopamine home, you are going to feel those benefits daily. This is very much down to individual taste and personality. There are, of course, people who would feel overstimulated by an excess of pattern and colour, but the key is finding what works to make you feel good, so that it will impact your general day-to-day mood and wellbeing positively.

As I will come back to again and again throughout this book, dopamine decor is really all about what makes you tick. Designer Kathy Kuo recommends thinking about 'the places, people and personal touchstones that make you feel most relaxed and content' as the starting place for your dopamine home journey. My home — and the examples of dopamine homes that you will see throughout this book — all reflect the unique personality and tastes of their owners. I hope you will draw inspiration from these spaces, but your own dopamine home will probably look entirely different…and that is exactly as it should be.

A Trend for Trying Times

To my mind, it surely seems too great a coincidence that at a time of rising global insecurity, a cost-of-living crisis and the after-effects of a pandemic, the trend of dopamine decor is on the rise. I am sure that, at a time of great challenge, many people, just like me, realized that their mental health and wellbeing have benefited from embracing the principles of dopamine decor.

I know this from personal experience: firstly, from living in our rented flat, which was tainted with sadness; and then during the renovation, while the house was very brown, very oppressive and utterly dreary (brown is definitely not one of my happy colours). We didn't feel content to be at home and always looked for excuses to be out. Now, I enter a room filled with colours I love and patterns that bring me happiness, and I can feel how dramatically my mood is altered. I feel the stress drain out of me; I'm in my happy place.

Find Your Tribe: Types of Dopamine Decor

One of the reasons I love dopamine decor is because it is so personal.

It's about what makes you happy and can be achieved easily by tuning into what gives you that warm, fuzzy feeling. This means there are many interpretations of the aesthetic: bold, eclectic, nostalgic, kitsch and pastel, to name a few.

Let's Get Quizzical

So, which style camp are you in? Reliving my teenage magazine days, on the next page you will find a fun quiz to help you find the trends that make you smile. Obviously, one size doesn't fit all — especially when it comes to dopamine decor — and you will likely find that you sit somewhere between two of the style camps. Starting out with a framework for how to approach your design can help to bring a cohesiveness to your home, which is a great way to ensure a harmonious and space-creating interior...plus, who doesn't love a quiz!?

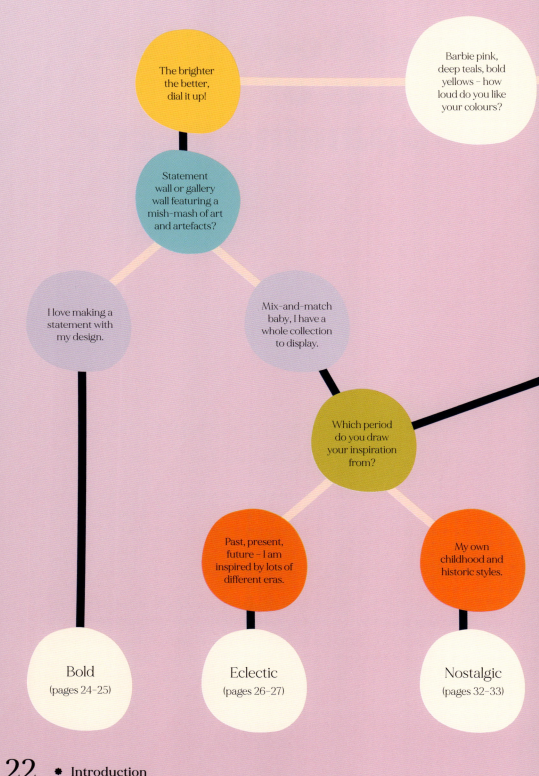

It's giving me a headache – softer tones are more my vibe.

Do you enjoy keeping trinkets from past dates and events?

Absolutely, I love collecting mementos of people, places and things.

Not overly, I am not too attached to bits and bobs.

Do you dream of Scandi-chic or Wes Anderson-style wonderland?

Wes Anderson sorbet shades for me.

Take me to Copenhagen!

Pastel
(pages 28–29)

Minimalism Meets Maximalism
(pages 30–31)

Find Your Tribe ◆ 23

Bold

This take on dopamine decor is a fearless deep-dive into bright tones, daring patterns and 'made you stop and stare' decor. Those who adopt this aesthetic aren't afraid to embrace the styles they love wholeheartedly.

Clockwise from top left: Bold and bright living room — Janine Genower (@houseofedencourt)

Fearless use of colour and pattern in Joanne Hardcastle's kitchen (@hardcastletowers)

Inspiration from Valspar for using paint to make an impact

Vivid dopamine-boosting living room — Laura Hall (@thehexagonalhouse)

Eclectic

These mood-boosting homes are a tantalizing blend of old and new, they are unique spaces that tap into the dopamine trend with ease. The exciting and unexpected details are perfect for stimulating dopamine.

Laura Hall (@thehexagonalhouse) has curated a sumptuous snug with rich colours, layers of texture and the perfect blend of old and new.

Pastel

Don't rule out pastels as childish, instead embrace the nostalgic feelings these pale tones can evoke. Think minty greens, lovely lilacs, lemon yellow, powder blues and sugary pinks. The Danish and Scandinavian pastel aesthetic has gained huge traction in recent years.

Clockwise from top left:
Pink and purple are the perfect pair — Helen Ford (@homewithhelenandco)

Popping pastel living room — Poppy Pearson (@letsgotopoppys)

Delicate pastels for a restful bedroom — Helen Ford (@homewithhelenandco)

Tranquil mint makes for a relaxing living space — Helen Ford (@homewithhelenandco)

Minimalism Meets Maximalism

Although dopamine decor is generally more in the maximalist camp, elements of minimalist design — such as sleek shapes and lines — lend themselves to a nice big dopamine fix.

Sleek lines combined with a bold use of pattern creates flow in an open-plan space.

Nostalgic

This style is all about finding those colours and cherished pieces that evoke childhood memories and take you back to a carefree, happy place, instantly releasing those powerful happy hormones. A perfect example of this is the resurgence in popularity of wavy lines, graphic prints and palettes rich in hues of mustard, amber and burnt orange, all of which are a homage to Seventies interior trends with its nod to disco and hippy culture.

Clockwise from top left:
Impeccable Art Deco bathroom — Nikki Shore (@weeny_victorian_house_in_ware)

Feeling groovy in Genie's lively lounge — Janine Genower (@houseofedencourt)

Warm colours and a range of art gives a homely vibe.

Find Your Tribe

Shoestring Decor

There can be a perception that maximalist aesthetics are more expensive, but this doesn't have to be the case.

My love of dopamine decor was born in an era when many have been feeling the effect of the cost-of-living crisis. I firmly believe that you should be able to have a beautiful, smile-inducing home on any budget, and with dopamine decor you absolutely can. After all, the trend is all about finding those personal touches, items that spark joy, and that can mean anything from thrift-shop finds to upcycled second-hand pieces. My personal take on the aesthetic is one that focuses on reusing and repurposing.

Top Five Budget-friendly Hacks for Creating a Dopamine Home

1. Thrift, Thrift, THRIFT!

I can't highlight the importance of this enough. Today, we live in a throw-away culture, and it is vitally important for us to try and change our habits around shopping. When we buy second hand, not only are we getting the feel-good factor from not trashing the planet, but there are so many unique gems out there that you can't buy in the stores or online.

Head to charity shops and furniture projects to source the best bargains. Go with a plan: it's easy to get overwhelmed or side-tracked, but if you know what you are looking for, you are more likely to have a successful outcome rather than return home with another three vases to add to the 'future-upcycle' pile. My number one tip for getting those top-tier second-hand finds is to persevere. Undoubtedly you will have unsuccessful days, but keep at it and the goods will turn up.

2. Go Online

Similarly to picking up those fab second-hand finds in the charity shops, you will find a whole world of treasure on sites such as Gumtree, eBay, Freecycle and — my personal go-to — Facebook Marketplace. People are often deterred by not finding the items they want on their first search, but my top tip is to train that algorithm to work for you. Save all the items you like and soon it will start to suggest items for you. Also, use specific search terms, such as 'mid-century' or 'retro', alongside the product you are looking for, to get better-tailored results.

The downside of buying online is that you can't get the first-hand look at the item's condition that you can when thrifting, so make sure to ask lots of questions. Especially about dimensions — you don't want to have your heart set on something only to discover it's too big to fit in your car, or it was in fact a dolls' house rug, which is why it was such a bargain!

One of my favourite upcycle projects: a thrifted tile coffee table given a new life with a lick of paint.

3. Use Leftovers

Again, this is a great way to avoid waste and it will save your wallet, too. Use leftover wallpaper for feature walls or small spaces such as under the stairs or loft hatches. Wallpaper is also great for upcycling: add fun to the inside or exterior of furniture, or even frame pieces as part of a unique gallery wall. Go wild with those leftover tins of paint and paint samples to add colour blocks to walls and to brighten up furniture. Use any excess tiles on unexpected surfaces to give a table or cabinet a new look. Bought too much timber? Make yourself a portable pagoda. Once you start thinking creatively, the world is your oyster.

4. Paint Everything

My love for paint is not purely for its transformative nature. Yes, it is by far the easiest way to switch up the look of a room, but it also gives you a lot of bang for your buck. I have painted everything from my kitchen appliances and radiators to upholstery and lampshades! It keeps costs down to use sample pots for smaller projects. Valspar paints are perfect for this as the samples are much bigger than your average size.

Another creative way to use emulsion is to paint your own wallpaper. Not only will you have produced a design unique to you, but it will be far cheaper than buying wallpaper.

It's a great way to use up leftover paints and sample pots, so don't hold back, use up all the colours you have collected over the years. If you are like me, you'll be spoiled for choice! You can paint your own pattern freehand, use tape to create checks or squares, or even repeatedly use a small stencil (such as flowers) to get a patterned wallpaper effect.

5. Do It Yourself

Of course, doing the hard graft yourself is one sure-fire way to save money. Understandably though, you might feel nervous about this. If you don't feel ready to embark on full renovations, try out the decorative side of things first. Painting and decorating yourself is usually fairly straightforward, even wallpapering can be picked up from DIY blogs or YouTube. Don't be put off trying out new projects due to a lack of tools either, it is easy and cost-effective to rent tools for a short period of time. So, jobs like sanding floors don't necessarily need a professional anymore.

Upcycling is a great way to save money, and it's better for the environment. A dusty and stained chair (left) was transformed by a lick of paint (right).

38 ◆ Introduction

PART ONE:

THE CORE PRINCIPLES OF DOPAMINE DECOR

Bold, Brave Colours

I'm not going to tell you that I woke up one day and designed my entire home in an uplifting, harmonious scheme.

It came with patience, a growth in confidence and a lot of trial and error. What I am going to do is give you the tips that I wish someone had given me, to help you to tap into the magical power of colour.

Colour is an integral part of a dopamine home, especially for me. As my home has become more colourful, I have felt happier. When choosing colours for my home, I found myself continually — and physically — being drawn to orange and peachy corals, which I now know are great for stimulating dopamine. Creating a home decorated in a beautiful, bold palette can mean enveloping yourself in a positive, mood-enhancing environment. Of course, the warming-spice hues that bring me unadulterated delight might not have the same effect on you; the way we react to colour is deeply personal. All it takes is a bad memory somehow entwined with a particular colour for it to make us run cold.

The Psychology of Colour

None of this is new or ground-breaking, colour theory has been around for centuries. Chromotherapy (as colour therapy is also known) was studied by the ancient civilizations of Egypt (where they believed that the use of colour for healing originated with the god Thoth), Greece and India. In each case, different colours were thought to be associated with particular needs, ailments or moods, and the application of these colours — in dyes, ointments, chakras, or otherwise — could provide a remedy.

The colour wheel has long been studied to help us understand the effect of colour on us, and it is the basis for how colours relate to each other. The colour wheel is made up of warm and cool colours. The warm colours (red, orange, yellow) are known to, quite literally, make us feel cosy and warm. As the US National Library of Medicine explains: 'The brain is largely devoted to making predictions. Since we have observed that red is associated to fire and hot temperatures, our brain may predict that a red object is going to have a warmer temperature than a blue object.'

While the colours I am most drawn to sit on the warm side of the colour wheel, I also have favourites on the cool side (purple, blue, green). In fact, my first true colour love, green, resides on that very side of the wheel that spans green through to purple. When we began our DIY journey, we kicked off with our kitchen reno; I was utterly clueless. I knew nothing except I had spotted a green tile that was making me feel a certain kind of way. That tile — which had so much depth, with all the jade and emerald jewel tones reflecting within it — was the starting point for the entire kitchen design. The cooler side of the wheel is known for its connection to nature and calmness, and I think our kitchen, with all the plants and wood, is definitely one of our most peaceful spaces.

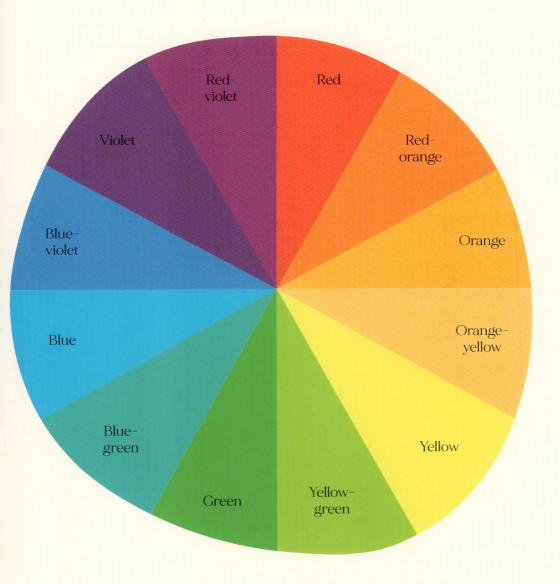

Bold, Brave Colours

> '*Colour is a power that directly influences the soul.*'
> – Wassily Kandinsky

Feel Your Way

According to colour psychology different colours affect our emotional responses, behaviours and mood. These reactions are understood to be due to psychological, cultural and personal reasons. The colours that sit most naturally within a dopamine home would veer towards the warmer side of the colour wheel, which has happy connotations, with a nice smattering of jewel colours from the cooler side. Pinks, reds, oranges and yellows symbolize energy, joy, love, hope and happiness. Greens and blues represent peace, growth, healing and nature. To reference Mental Health America, 'bright, warm colours are best in rooms for entertaining like dining rooms or kitchens' to stimulate feelings of happiness and joy, while 'cool tones' are excellent for 'relaxing spaces' like bedrooms and bathrooms, to evoke a sense of calm and quiet.

However, it's important to understand that your subjective emotional and cultural responses can alter your experiences of different colours and the psychological impact they can have. For example, if you had a terrible experience on holiday where you stayed in a room that was bright yellow, and that experience has impacted your visceral response to yellow, there will be no way that colour makes it into your happy-home palette. Have a think about the colours that really speak to you and make your heart sing – this is one of the fundamental principles of dopamine decor.

Bold, Brave Colours

Reds and Pinks

Red is synonymous with passion and danger. It is an intense colour that you wouldn't necessarily think is a natural fit with interiors, but a fiery pop of red – as seen with 'the unexpected red theory' – works surprisingly well. The theory, coined by designer Taylor Migliazzo Simon on TikTok, demonstrates that the boldness of adding a red tone or accessory to a room will enhance your interior design. By using this technique, red becomes a colour you can use in most rooms, meaning it's not so scary after all.

Pink, of course, is an offshoot of red and despite some people having reservations about it being 'immature' or 'girly', notions that I hate, it is a tone that is very easily incorporated into the home. You don't have to opt for full bright Barbie pink (unless that makes you happy, in which case, go for it!), there is a whole world of pastel, rose and dusky pinks to explore, which will create a nurturing and inviting interior.

Top left and bottom right: Delivering the unexpected red theory perfectly throughout her home – Steph Nicholson (@houseonthecorner_16)

Top right: Dusty pinks can create a warm, sophisticated vibe.

Bottom left: Bright red accessories can deliver a pop of colour.

Shoestring Tip

The unexpected red theory is a great shoestring tip — the whole idea is based on how the addition of even the smallest and most unlikely touch of red in a room can enliven the whole space, especially in places where it enhances the existing palette. You could easily add an affordable accessory such as a cushion, lampshade or even prints with shades of red. Or turn to your trusty paint brush and give an old piece of furniture a red makeover. I have seen red wooden chairs, stools, fireplaces and even bathtubs that have really pulled a space together.

Orange and Coral

The joy of orange ranges from rich russet to soft apricot with so many delicious tones in between. It is a cheerful and stimulating colour, one that I am drawn back to time and time again. If you are new to using orange in your home and you don't feel confident to embrace a vibrant tone yet, the lighter peachy hues make an excellent wall colour for nearly all rooms — they work especially well to create a warm, welcoming hallway.

As a personal favourite from this part of the colour wheel, I need to give coral a special mention. Coral, named after the magical marine invertebrates, blends orange and pink on the colour wheel, and the sizzling vibrancy it brings to a home is guaranteed to elevate any space. It pops perfectly against darker rooms, and its orange roots mean that it pairs beautifully with gold. Coral is definitely a colour I would recommend trying if you are just starting out and dipping a toe into your colourful home journey.

Top left: Orange and green make a lovely, fresh pairing.

Top right: Liven up any room with a zesty orange wall colour.

Bottom left: Go bold in unexpected rooms.

Bottom right: My favourite orange sofa.

Yellows

Yellow is the colour of sunshine and it quite literally brings warmth to a space. The spectrum ranges from light lemony hues all the way to earthy mustard tones. Of course, it's not going to be everyone's cup of tea. According to textile designer Rebecca Atwood, in her book *Living with Colour*, 'the human eye is quite sensitive to yellow'. This could explain the varied emotions that the tone awakens in us. Personally, I adore a bright pop of yellow, it not only adds vibrant cosiness but also a sense of fun. It's great in kids' bedrooms, as well as an uplifting accent throughout your home.

Top left: A slice of sunshine happiness in Genie's kitchen — Janine Genower (@houseofedencourt)

Right: Pantone for H&M provides bold yellow pops, perfect for brightening a space.

Bottom left: Gold tones can give a grown-up take on yellows.

'How lovely yellow is! It stands for the sun.'

– Vincent van Gogh

'Remember, green's your colour. You are spring.'
– Gwendolyn Brooks

Greens

Green is rooted in a connection to nature and its calming tones lend it well to rooms to relax in, such as bedrooms. It also symbolizes new beginnings and can be refreshing and revitalizing, so it works well in bathrooms, while deep, forest greens can create a sumptuous look in a snug, study or lounge. Green might not be a colour you have felt drawn to, but it's worth opening your eyes to all the different hues from pastel mint to deep, dark teals — you may well surprise yourself by discovering a new love.

Top left: Fresh green on kitchen cabinets brightens a space.

Top right: Olive tones are restful for a bedroom...

Bottom right: ...while dark greens can create a dramatic and stylish space.

Bottom left: Neon green accessories are a fun addition.

Blues

I wholeheartedly believe there is a blue for every situation, so even if it might not be your first colour choice there is a chance you might find a shade to suit you and your home. Need a dark and dramatic backdrop to make your decor pop? Navy has got you with her blue-black tones. Want a bright, fresh space? Icy powder blue is the answer. Fancy a joyous burst of sheer happiness? Let me introduce you to cornflower. The versatility of blue is definitely a factor in the colour's popularity. Blue not only looks incredible in virtually all spaces, but it also makes us feel good. Often, we find ourselves soothed by nature, in particular the sea and sky, both of which are mirrored by the blue spectrum (well, on a good day) and this adds to the peace we feel when we are surrounded by blue.

Top left: Lick Blue 111 – just one of many gorgeous blue shades to choose from.

Top right: Bedroom with a stunning sky blue ceiling – Julie Choi (@letsby.avenue)

Bottom right: Dark blue has dramatic impact when used in a space.

Purples

Being close to blue on the colour wheel, purple shares many of the same traits. Just as blue can create a calm and tranquil environment, so too can shades of purple. Perhaps because of the colour's historical links to royalty, purple evokes decadence. While some may find an indulgent darker purple overstimulating for rooms such as a bedroom, tones such as lilac and lavender are ideal for these spaces. Save the bolder tones for striking accents, or for creating an opulent moody look in an office or lounge.

Top left: Lovely lilac is perfect for a kid's bedroom — Shona East (@honeyjoyhome)

Top right: Lilac and peach make an invigorating pairing — Julie Choi (@letsby.avenue)

Middle right: Lick Purple 03 delivers deep, rich tones for a dramatic statement.

Bottom left: Pink and purple tones can be playful and glamourous.

Neutrals

To let you in on a secret, I was always jealous of people who can 'do' neutrals. I love an interior that uses creamy and rich neutrals — think caramels, pewter, ivory. These neutral tones can create homes that feel mature, balanced and comfortable. If, like me, you love neutrals but they just aren't really you, don't forget that these beige, sand and grey tones make excellent foundations for the more vibrant hues that you are drawn to.

Top left: Boutique hotel vibes incoming.

Top right: Calm and cosy kitchen — Laura Davies (@leopard_print_stairs)

Bottom right: Warm neutrals are restful and comforting.

Middle left: Neutral definitely doesn't mean dull — Glen Handley (@inside.number.twelve)

'White is the most wonderful colour because within it you can see all the colours of the rainbow.'

– Richard Meier

White

Surprisingly, many of my favourite dopamine homes actually have white walls. This not only helps all the art and accessories pop, but also means you have the freedom to change up decor easily without repainting, as very little clashes with white. When we think of white there can be a tendency to consider it bland and without personality. However, from that one shade there is a vast array of hues, from warm whites with red and orange undertones to those with the cooler blue and green tones, all subtle variations on the classic staple. White might not be the shade that immediately springs to mind when you decide to decorate, but far from being boring it can add a clean and fresh vibe to your home and is the ideal backdrop to let your decor dazzle.

Top left: The perfect colour for adding plenty of pattern — Laura Davies (@leopard_print_stairs)

Top right: Gorgeous green can take centre stage with a white backdrop — Carla Elliman (@carlaelliman)

Bottom right: Let's be honest, no one has eyes for anything other than the leopard print stairs — Laura Davies (@leopard_print_stairs)

Bottom left: White walls means no holding back on fun accessories — Charlotte Cannon (@homeofcharl)

Finding Your Colour Style

Over the years, I've repeatedly read that the colours in your wardrobe can be a good starting point to inspire your home-decor choices, and for many this is a great way to help initially identify the colours you're most drawn to. However, if you're anything like me and your closet is filled with various iterations of black, don't panic! It's not necessarily time to enter your modern gothic interior era just yet. Instead, look to art, nature, print and designs that leave you feeling energized and excited.

It might be your favourite pink peony in your family's garden, a thrifted Seventies-style bedspread or the colours of a dramatic sunset — inspiration can be drawn from anywhere. It's simply about tapping into how these things make you *feel*, and which colours boost your mood. When I spot something that I love, I always take a quick snap and jot down a note about what it was and how it made me feel, you can then use these later in moodboards (see page 66).

Eye-catching Colours

A great way to identify which colour combinations excite you and bring you pleasure is to go around your home gathering objects that you are drawn to. It could be your pink handbag, an orange bangle or a yellow vase. Consider the relationship between the colours you have collected and how they make you feel: do they elevate your energy in a harmonious way, or is the colour clash causing you a headache? Be led by what catches your eye and this will help you narrow down palettes if you feel overwhelmed. It's then easy to experiment by swapping colours in and out, as you simply replace objects that you have collected with others in a different colour.

The Perils of Social Media

You can find endless inspiration online via sources such as Pinterest and Instagram, which are brilliant to help you identify the colours you love and to visualize how they could look in a home. It's one thing knowing you love that pop of peony pink, but when you look at images of a room with that colour scheme, does it bring you the same joy? Be wary though, online can be a minefield; it's easy to be overwhelmed, or to be led away from your gut instincts and to follow a trend instead. I speak from personal experience and have fallen foul of this myself. Having spent far too much time oogling pretty, pastel dopamine homes on social media, I decided to upcycle a cute set of draws in lilac. I did give it my trademark pop of orange, with a stencilled flower pattern, and the colours were an absolutely perfect pairing. But did they work in my home where there is not even one tiny spec of lilac? Nope. They stood out like a sore thumb and, as much as I loved them, they had to go. So, the lesson I've learned so that you don't have to, is to stick to your gut feelings rather than following trends. A colour scheme that gives you a fuzzy glow will always do that, a trend you hopped on because you saw it on social media will quickly run its course and leave you itching to redecorate.

Practice Makes Perfect

Once you have identified a new hue or palette that you are drawn to, test it out. Instead of going full throttle and spending hours upcycling something that will never fit the flow of your home, find a smaller item (or items) in the shades you are considering and live with them in the space for a couple of weeks to get a feel for how well they work.

Remember though, even after you have researched, planned, designed and tested, things can sometimes still go wrong – and that's OK. If the completed space doesn't leave you excited, then it's easily fixed. Things can be repainted. Chalk it up to experience, they don't say you learn from your mistakes for no reason!

Once you have identified the colours that lift your mood, and start to be braver with your colour choices, you will find everything begins to fall into place. From one room with a beautifully curated palette will blossom another. As you are instinctively drawn to colours, these will appear repeatedly throughout your home and give the space a cohesive flow. For me there is a thread of green underpinning my home, with pops of orange, pink and coral throughout.

Make Mine a Moodboard

A moodboard is a design tool that helps you to experiment and visualize.

Using a moodboard helps you to gather ideas and see how they flow together — this will be the point where you will spot anything that doesn't work in your scheme. You can include inspirational images of furniture, scraps of wallpaper or fabric swatches. This is where your colour inspiration will really start to come to life to help you fine-tune your palette.

Moodboards can be created in stages, across apps and with physical samples. A great starting point is a vision board. **A vision board** is less about the design you are looking to create and more about honing in on what you are drawn to and what makes you tick. You can go all out here, including whatever makes you happy, from outfits and old CD covers to pressed flowers or quotes, it can be literally anything. If you are already very in touch with what you like, you can probably skip straight to the concept stage.

The next step is the **concept board**, this will draw inspiration from your vision board — which will have helped you to identify colours and textures you love — and start to become more of a design concept. These are generally best with either cut-out pictures or images collected electronically. Like the vision board, don't hold back. Yes, House of Hackney wallpaper is way out of budget, as is that dreamy Jonathan Adler sofa, but pop them down on your concept board anyway.

Next, go away and do your research. Find affordable versions of your dream scenario, or figure out a way to thrift or make your own version. And if your dream scenario is already something that fits your budget, even better.

Now to create your **moodboard**, this is the more practical stage and the tool to help you make final decisions. Creating this out of actual physical samples rather than an electronic collage works best but, of course, you can combine the two mediums if that's what you prefer. With a physical moodboard, not only can you see how the paint samples and fabric swatches respond to the light in your intended room, but you can also switch things in-and-out easily to discover the best combination. The moodboard will bring your vision and concept alive, aid decision making, and allow you to test if your design elements are harmonious.

Colour Palettes

Colour inspiration can be found in all walks of life, from the natural world to online.

Once you begin to identify the colours that give you the feel-good factor, then a colour palette is where you start to collate them — think of it as an interior design recipe, gathering the perfect ingredients to come together and make a delicious dish.

Typically, interior designers suggest that the ideal number of colours for a palette is between three and five. I'm not necessarily a big follower of rules, but in general your palette will be made up of one main anchor colour (i.e., the central colour you're most attracted to), one to three neutral(s) (which don't have to be beige, but rather paired-down hues of your anchor colour), and an accent colour.

Charlotte Cannon's living room has a perfectly planned palette — (@homeofcharl)

Sample Palettes

On the following pages are some example colour schemes, a couple of which I have used around my own home. I have listed the original paint brands for each paint colour, but for the more expensive options I have always used Valspar paint match, and I have never been disappointed by the quality of the paint. You will see lots of crossover between the palettes. This means that there is then a cohesive colour story woven throughout your home. It is also more affordable as you can use the leftover paint in other spaces or for touch ups.

✶ The Core Principles of Dopamine Decor

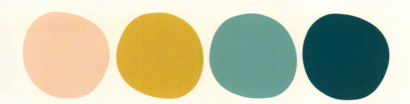

Palette 1:
Let's Go to the Beach

These natural sea and sand tones are the perfect relaxing palette for a bedroom. I have these blue-greens in my bedroom and they are hues that are beautifully complemented by accents of golds, pinks and oranges.

- Farrow & Ball Wevet
- Claybrook Studio Peach Juice
- Valspar Sunset Spice
- Valspar Pastoral Peace
- Valspar Fish Tale

Palette 2:
Sophisticated Glam

Muted pinks and deep blues make for a grown-up palette that feels both restful and glamorous. Perfect for a dining room space.

- Farrow & Ball Hague Blue
- Valspar Skyscraper
- Lick Red 03
- Farrow & Ball Pink Ground
- Farrow & Ball Wevet

Palette 3:
Botanical Boss

This green and pink palette is a nod to my love of all things botanical, with greens ranging from dark to muted.

- Farrow & Ball Wevet
- Valspar Brushed Cotton
- Valspar On Pointe
- Valspar Rugged Olive
- Valspar L'Escargot

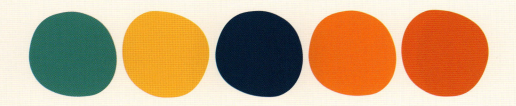

Palette 4:
Retro Rainbow

This is a bold colour scheme that lends itself perfectly to a modern living space.

- Valspar Aussie Surf
- Valspar Flemish Tapestry
- Farrow & Ball Hague Blue
- Valspar Outre Orange
- Valspar Sandy Peppers

Palette 5:
Grown-up Pastel

Pastels can sometimes be associated with cute or childlike spaces. This doesn't have to be the case, and by adding an almost grubby green to a pretty pastel palette you can create a grown-up take on pastels that would work well in any room.

- Farrow & Ball Yeabridge Green
- Valspar You Are My Sunshine
- Valspar Air Dry
- Valspar Vintage Peach
- Valspar Like a Boss

Palette 6:
Unexpected Red

The pop of red against this cool blue palette is the equivalent of the perfect red lippy finishing off your outfit. It completes the sophisticated look. This is a collection of colours that would look perfect in a living room or snug.

- Farrow & Ball Hague Blue
- Farrow & Ball Chinese Blue
- Farrow & Ball Wevet
- Valspar Sandy Peppers
- Valspar Air Dry

Colour Palettes ❋ 75

Palette 7:
Spice Up Your Life

This warm and welcoming palette has earthy hues which immediately lift your spirits. The invigorating tones are ideally suited to a study, but would work well across the whole home, including children's bedrooms.

- Valspar Sandy Peppers
- Valspar Outre Orange
- Farrow & Ball Pink Ground
- Valspar Flemish Tapestry
- Farrow & Ball Yeabridge Green

Palette 8:
Blue and Green SHOULD Be Seen

Whoever came up with the famous 'blue and green' rhyme got it absolutely the wrong way round! I love the harmonious way blue and green work together. There isn't really any space in your home where blue and green won't work, as you will find with this calming and considered palette.

- Valspar Air Dry
- Farrow & Ball Breakfast Room Green
- Farrow & Ball Wevet
- Farrow & Ball Chinese Blue
- Valspar Brushed Cotton

The pop of red completes this colour scheme — Steph Nicholson (@houseonthecorner_16)

The Magic of Paint

Paint is my favourite decorative medium, without a shadow of a doubt.

Not just for its sheer transformative nature but for ease of application, too. It's affordable and it's massively impactful. I also love that it can be changed or changed back relatively quickly. Take it from someone who once painted a white ceiling bright red, quickly realized the error of my ways, painted it back white and then finally settled on a deep teal. All in thirty-six hours!

The possibilities with paint are endless. I have been known to paint chequered ceilings, colour blocks, retro murals and stripes. And it's not just for walls. From colour drenching a room including ceiling, radiators, coving and skirting to painting appliances and patios. It really is one of the quickest and easiest ways to inject bold and beautiful colour into your home.

We are incredibly lucky that we live in an age where there are so many types of paint available, a fun day out to me is a trip to my local DIY or home improvement store to peruse the paint samples. I'm a huge fan of colour matching and am forever taking scraps of wallpaper, fabric or photos in to get the perfect pigment custom made for me.

To anyone looking to get started on a dopamine home, I would always say that paint is the easiest place to start, so forget the fear and pick up that brush!

Which Paint Where?

Although I refer to painting as 'quick and easy', I do recognize that it can be daunting. Especially with the sheer variety of paints out there and not knowing which sort might suit what surface, so here is a quick guide to the various paints available and what to use them for.

Primers are often in-built to paints nowadays, especially furniture paint, but there is still a place for primers. In my experience, Zinsser primer is an absolute miracle product. It means paint adheres to even the trickiest surface (melamine springs to mind). It's also great for stain blocking. It's on the expensive side but worth every penny, and one tin will last you many projects.

The paint finish describes how matte or glossy a paint will appear. Once you have decided on the colour, it's time to consider what finish will work best in your space. It's worth considering both aesthetics and practicalities when you choose your finish as some are more durable than others.

GLOSS PAINT is the most shiny paint finish, giving a polished look.

Best for decorative features and a popular choice for bathroom or kitchen cabinets. I've also seen gloss ceilings, which reflect the light beautifully.

SATIN PAINT is probably my favourite finish. It sits in the middle of matte and gloss. The slight reflective nature can help make a space feel bigger.

Best for most spaces, it is both versatile and durable. It's also easy to clean, so perfect for all the small fingerprints on our walls!

EGGSHELL is very similar in appearance to satin, just with less sheen.

Best for walls and ceilings. It can also be used on some furniture and radiators.

MATTE PAINT is often known as 'flat' or 'flat matte'. It has a finish with no sheen and is velvety in appearance.

Best for rooms with less traffic as it is not easily cleaned, and can scuff and mark more easily.

Specialist paints are available for pretty much every surface these days. If you want to paint tiles, wood, metal or furniture, you will find a paint out there for you.

My first recommendation is Rust-oleum who really do have a paint for everything, their Universal All-Surface paint is fantastic and they have a brilliant range of specialist paints for tiles, radiators, kitchen cupboards and even a furniture paint that requires no sanding or removal of any previous paint job. As someone who loathes prep, it doesn't get any better than that!

My second go-to is Valspar, they do not have quite such an extensive range of specialist paints, but stock furniture, wood, metal and masonry, and in my opinion, they are unmatched in colour choice. A colour from their range paired with Zinsser primer, and there's not much you won't be able to paint.

The Magic of Paint

My Top Five Painting Tips

Although, as I've mentioned, I loathe prep, it is essential for achieveing a brilliant paint finish. Take your time, do the job properly, and you won't regret it. Below are my top tips for professional-grade painting.

1. Prep is Key

Yes, we would all love to be painting directly onto a perfectly smooth, freshly plastered wall, but in reality, we are probably redecorating a surface that has lingering marks and holes from shelves and screws. So, your first task will be to fill and sand these to give you the smoothest base to start on. Even if there are no holes to fill, if the previous paint is gloss or satin, it would be good practice to give the walls a sand. Once your walls are clean and dry, it's time to get out those protective sheets and make sure everything is covered up.

2. Prime for Best Coverage

If you are painting over a dark colour, a stain or, in my case, a giant rainbow mural, then using a primer is a good call. Otherwise, you are probably fine to skip this stage.

3. Roll On

Use a roller and this will make light work of the rest of the space.

4. Cut in With Confidence

If you aren't confident, or don't have a steady hand, then use tape to ensure straight edges. Go round light switches, plugs, skirting and coving. FrogTape is hands down the best that I have come across and they do a range of tapes for different surfaces. Paint using a brush or roller, and make sure to reapply tape between coats rather than leave the tape on for too long in case it pulls off paint when you remove it. If you are more confident in your abilities to paint a straight line, get a really good precision paint brush to aid you with cutting in. I am all for saving money but in the case of paint brushes it is money well spent to buy decent ones, we love Harris brushes in our house.

5. Don't Skirt the Issue

If you are painting skirting boards, my number one tip is to make sure they are spotless! Being so near to the floor means they collect more dust than other areas, and the last thing you want is lots of little bumps and bobbles adorning your freshly painted skirting board.

To Paint or Not to Paint?

There is literally nothing I wouldn't try painting! But in general, you will want to avoid sockets and light switches. Radiators can look great painted in a cool contrast colour, or colour drenched to match the walls (see page 132). Doors and doorframes are also an opportunity to make a style statement, if you wish. Contrasting frames and colourful doors add a fun, quirky touch to a room.

The Magic of Paint ● 83

Get Touchy-feely

Just in the way that colour can influence our moods and feelings, so too can the textures and textiles around us.

When we come into physical contact with something that gives us pleasure, it instantly stimulates those feel-good hormones. Think back to a time where you've run your hands through a deliciously textured blanket or slipped your feet into a brand-new pair of comforting slippers that instantly sparked joy.

Comparable to how colour therapy has taught us that certain colours can evoke different emotional responses (see page 46), the same can be said for textures. Smooth marble, glass or steel might suggest cool and calm, whereas velvet, cashmere, wood and wool stimulate cosiness and warmth.

Incorporating Tactile Elements for Comfort

One way to harness the power of texture therapy is to create a tactile experience by layering lots of soft and snuggly textures. A bed made up with silky sheets, fluffy pillows and a downy throw will instantly become a safe and restful sanctuary.

Using deep plush rugs or carpets that tantalize your toes will stimulate feelings of pleasure and, when juxtaposed against stunning tiles or flooring, heighten those physical and emotional responses to your surroundings. A velvet sofa, like my favourite orange one, will never fail to create a feeling of comfort. When combined with varying textured and coloured cushions, there is no place I would rather snuggle.

Also, don't forget that in summer months or warmer climes those cooling fabrics – such as linen and cotton, and beautiful billowing voile curtains – are equally important for comfort.

How to Select Soft Furnishings That Spark Joy

Soft furnishings are the perfect opportunity to embrace texture therapy. Cushions, rugs, throws and bedding are already pliable and comfortable, you just need to elevate them to the next level by incorporating the psychology of dopamine decor to make them work even harder for you. The key to this is making sure you are selecting pieces that spark joy. Start with the basics: tap into your gut instincts, your physical draw to certain colours, patterns and textures, and make sure you select pieces based on your emotional response to them.

The most impactful soft furnishings are rugs and bedding. Cushions and throws are wonderful for bringing in different colours, patterns and textures, but bedding and rugs take up a greater space in the home and you have more physical contact with them. To create an uplifting environment, make the most of the mood-boosting properties of those tactile soft furnishings.

Shoestring Tip

For a quick, cost-effective interior switch up, look to the humble rug. I have a whole collection of rugs, which I use on rotation. They are such a fantastic way to quickly adjust the look and feel of a room. You can change them seasonally — a deep, shaggy pile for autumn/winter and sleek and soft for spring/summer. Or just change them on a whim when you fancy a new stimulating environment. When they aren't in use, I simply roll them up, wrap in bin bags and slide under my sofas and beds. You wouldn't wear the same shoes all year round, so think of your soft furnishings in the same way. Keep a stash of staples that spark joy to mix-and-match depending on the season, your mood or fancy!

Get Touchy-feely

Embrace Pattern

Embracing patterns is key to creating a dopamine home.

    Bold elements such as wallpaper, painted murals and eclectic art have always been my go-to for injecting a big dose of dopamine via pattern. However, you don't need to limit your use to the walls; flooring is often a hugely neglected space. Forget grey carpets, seize the opportunity and go all out with rugs, which come in a vast array of delicious patterns. And don't overlook tiles with all the beautiful designs available, from traditional Dutch to colourful Moroccan-style, bold geometric patterns to Victorian florals. If tiles are slightly out of your budget or feel too permanent, have a go at recreating a similar look with paints and a stencil. We stencilled our patio with a striking design and it is quite honestly one of the best decisions we made, it has elevated the space beyond my wildest hopes.

Wallpaper is another great option to consider when trying to bring fresh and bold patterns into your home; it can dramatically change a space. If you feel slightly daunted by the idea, my biggest tip is to start small. You don't need to wallpaper a whole room, simply start by choosing an area you want to be a feature — such as the walls either side of a fireplace or behind your bed — and have a go. And don't feel limited to walls: wallpapered ceilings are making a huge comeback. The most exciting thing about wallpaper is the limitless possibilities, there are so many designs out there. Find one that makes your heart sing!

Shoestring Tip

If you are craving the grown-up glamour of tiles without the price tag, or have old tiles in need of a refresh, there is an ever-increasing range of self-adhesive tiles available as a DIY-friendly option. Most options come in a range of standard tile sizes, and you can order the quantity required for your space. Each will have its own application guidelines, but as a rule you will need to prepare the surface by giving it a good clean and making sure it is completely dry before carefully applying the stick-on tiles. Most are waterproof and suitable for kitchen and bathroom areas — always check before you buy and read the reviews from other customers to make sure it will stand up in the area you want to use it.

Pattern as a Starting Point

Over the years, many of the design schemes around my home have stemmed from a particular pattern. From a much-loved print or wallpaper, I have drawn out the colours and my scheme is born.

Pattern is something that has always inspired me; my living room colour scheme was born from a lovely John Lewis wallpaper I spotted, 'Ipanema'. The grey-blue tropical foliage design with subtle toucans peeping out at me and the mustard gold flecks, captivated me. I chose my Hague Blue walls to make it pop and had a Valspar colour-match paint made up as the exact grey-blue of the foliage to paint my mantel. From that one wallpaper many more botanical patterns have blossomed.

One of the best things about pattern is just how subjective and personal they can be: one pattern that fills someone with joy, might be another person's nightmare! It's about tapping into your unique physical and emotional response to a particular pattern and testing to see how it could work in your home.

Make it Flow

The fear of overwhelming a space with patterns is often what holds people back from using them in the home. One of the best ways to create a harmonious home with an abundance of pattern is to mirror shapes and patterns throughout the space. For instance, in my dining room I have a pretty full-on mural, which is a palm print. Rather than play it safe and pick a single colour to mirror in my rug choice, I took it a step further and found a rug that not only matched the tones of the mural, but also had a slight botanical print. Far from overpowering the space, it tied everything together harmoniously. I have a similar botanical wallpaper in the lounge that I often match to floral rugs. The theme of plants and flowers is one that underpins my whole home, which also helps to create a cohesive feeling.

Five Easy Ways to Start With Pattern in Your Home

1. Start Small

It's not just the fear of making the wrong design choices for aesthetic reasons, but we can also worry about the financial repercussions of making the wrong choices. While building your confidence with pattern experimentation, it's probably not wise to dash out and splash your hard-earned cash on an expensive statement piece that you may live to regret. Ease yourself into pattern gradually with smaller items. Think cushions, throws and art as simple ways to get going on your pattern journey.

2. Add Layers

You might not feel ready yet for a ditsy print chair against a backdrop of striped wallpaper, but how about an assortment of patterned cushions against a statement sofa? This is one way to dip your toe into the layering of patterns. Personal favourite combinations of mine are a few plain velvet cushions mixed in with some striped ones, a flower print and an unusual shape. A good way to keep the patterns harmonious is to have similar colours underpinning the look.

3. Look to Soft Furnishings

Adding a patterned headboard or bedding is a really easy and effective way to add pattern to a bedroom. Beautiful bedding can be picked up relatively cheaply these days with everyone from Primark to supermarkets selling fun, vibrant sets. You can upcycle your old plain headboard without difficulty using a staple gun and whatever fabric has taken your fancy (see page 188).

4. **Try a Focal Piece**

As I said earlier, don't blow all your savings, but maybe try a thrifted patterned chair, a lamp with a quirky lampshade or a dramatic footstool. Before you know it, it will have snowballed, and you will be adding more patterned decor that you spot complements the focal piece.

5. **Don't Forget the Floor**

Floors are huge spaces crying out for patterns! The large expanse lends itself perfectly to a statement piece, but if you aren't feeling that brave there are lots of very cool checked, striped or scalloped rugs that can add interest. I am always blown away by the sheer variety out there and if you can't pick just one, you can create a unique layered look with multiple rugs.

Embrace Pattern

Bring the Outside In

One easy way to weave nature into your decor is through colour.

Sea and sky blues, all of nature's splendid greens and earthy tones — these are colours that will bring warmth and tranquillity into your home. As well as embracing tones from the natural world, there are many fabulous botanical patterns and prints that will also give the impression of bringing the outdoors inside. Since I was a child, my favourite subjects to paint and draw have always been flowers and plants. I love everything about them: the colours, the delicacy, the fact they are to be enjoyed so briefly in their temporary, fleeting beauty. I have tapped into this passion and the joy that flowers give me in my decor — all of the wallpapers in my home are botanical or floral.

Go Green

To me, the very best way to harness the power of the natural world within your home is to fill it with plants and greenery. I have learned over time that I am not particularly green fingered, but I know how happy it makes me to have plants in the home, so I have persevered. There is nothing like a gorgeous pop of greenery to lift a drab corner.

Like with finding the colours and decor that work for you, it's about finding the plants you are best suited to. One favourite of mine is the trusty, near-indestructible pothos (*Epipremnum aureum*), also known as devil's ivy. I especially love that they are trailing plants, so look very dramatic hanging vertically down from shelves – they can also be trained to grow across walls. Pothos come in a vast array of different greens, and I refuse to believe there isn't a person out there who wouldn't feel a bit happier from having a zingy neon pothos in their home.

Life would be boring without a little variety though, wouldn't it? So, if you're totally averse to even the most unkillable plants, faux plants are an excellent alternative that are cost-friendly in the long run. Many of the faux plants on the market are of incredible quality and totally undetectable!

Plant shelves offer another gorgeous way to add fun to a room; they work especially well in bathrooms, where many plants thrive, as well as in kitchens. You can't go wrong with a big palm or fiddle-leaf fig in a statement pot, and I also love a terrarium, which is currently making a comeback from its Seventies heyday.

The best thing about harnessing the magical power of plants and creating a calming mood-boosting oasis is that they are so easy to include in your decor, it truly is as easy as popping a plant onto a shelf!

Bring the Outside In

My Top Five (Nearly) Unkillable Plants

1. Pothos
(*Epipremnum aureum*)

My go-to plant, which has never let me down, the faithful pothos is also known as devil's ivy. This plant strikes me as more saintly than demonic given the amount of abuse she will patiently endure, over- or under-water and 99 per cent of the time she will survive. This plant is for anyone wanting to be in that cool plant-parent gang, but simply doesn't have the time to commit.

2. Peace Lily
(*Spathiphyllum wallisii*)

The peace lily is the only plant that has ever graced me with a flower! Despite being on the needy side, she is a surprisingly tough cookie. She is prone to wilt dramatically when she needs attention, a sure-fire way to make sure she gets the watering she needs. No withering away quietly like a cheese plant for this one, which means she is far more likely to survive in the hands of those with less than green fingers.

3. Parlour Palm
(*Chamaedorea elegans*)

The parlour palm is my sort of plant: she gives fancy vibes, but she's no diva. According to houseplant experts, Patch Plants, she received her common name in Victorian times: 'For Victorians, the parlour was the best room in the house, where you would receive your fanciest visitors and display your fanciest possessions. This exotic palm would suggest you were worldly and sophisticated'. The fact you can appear worldly and sophisticated without putting in many plant-care hours endears me all the more to this resilient plant.

3

4. Snake Plant (*Sansevieria*)

An ideal option if, like me, you are prone to forgetting that plants need water to survive. Luckily the snake plant thrives in dry conditions so won't hold the lack of H_2O against you and will keep delivering that much needed greenery into your home.

5. Cactus (family Cactaceae)

And if all else fails don't forget there is always the trusty stalwart, the cactus! There is a huge range of these hardy plants to choose from, in all different shapes and sizes. Cowboy chic is all the rage, so your decidedly ungreen fingers are doing you a favour here!

Bring the Outside In ❋ 99

Keep It Clean

A number of scientific studies have proven that clutter disrupts our mental health, contributing to feelings of stress and overwhelm – the antithesis of the dopamine home!

According to *Psychology Today* clutter 'can interrupt your flow — both your ability to move and your ability to *think*'. When we are surrounded by mess, we become distracted, making it harder for us to focus on tasks and more prone to procrastination. Far from our home being a place of relaxation and comfort, too much clutter can make it a source of stress and frustration.

So, in order to keep a happy, healthy mind, keeping your home and treasures as organized as possible is essential.

Everything in its Place

Organized doesn't have to mean everything hidden and sterile, you can still have all your best beautiful bits out on display, but everything should have its place.

Ample storage is key to keeping a clutter-free home and there are endless solutions that can be an attractive addition to your home, such as sweet baskets for toys, built-in, floor-to-ceiling cupboards, blanket boxes with a funky print, and retro bookshelves. When considering your options, make sure you think practically (see page 105), but consider aesthetics, too. Storage, when done well, can meld seamlessly into your decor, and even add to the personal warmth of a room, showing off all your treasured items while keeping the rest safely stashed away.

I am a big fan of open shelving in my bathroom and kitchen as I can style them with plants, candles and prints. I also make sure there are spaces for pretty storage jars of practical items, too — tea bags and spices in the kitchen, and cotton buds and bath bombs in the bathroom. You can find a balance between looking good and keeping it functional. As long as that 'clutter' has a home, you won't have that overwhelmed, anxious feeling that you can get when there is 'stuff everywhere'.

> 'Having a simplified, uncluttered home is a form of self-care.'
> – Emma Scheib

The Clear Out

Of course, storage is great for keeping your home neat, tidy and stress-free, but there will be a limit on how much you can cram into your newly organized drawers and arrange on your stylish shelves. If you have a huge home, you can probably afford to be less ruthless, but for the many of us who struggle with storage solutions even for the essentials, it might be time to get Marie 'if it doesn't spark joy' Kondo on your possessions.

I am not suggesting you be quite as extreme as to get rid of anything that doesn't make you happy, I mean we still all need a loo brush, but it is a good idea not to hold onto everything forever and to make sure your home is organized.

Storage Checklist

When considering what storage you need for your home, make sure you answer these questions first:

- **What do you need to store?** Think about the size, quantity and nature of the objects.

- **How accessible does it need to be?** There is nothing more frustrating than having to empty and entire basket to get to the pair of shoes you need. Sure, it looks pretty, but will it work on a day-to-day basis?

- **...Or not be?** Some items you want to store may need to be kept safely away from little hands or pet's paws.

- **Can I make it work harder?** Storage doesn't just have to be a cupboard taking up space. Think inventively about how to make it work best for you. Shoe storage in the hallway that doubles up as a place to sit; sofas with hidden storage under the chairs. Use those wasted spaces as well — behind-the-door solutions can be clever and stylish for small bathrooms or bedrooms, and shelves above radiators are another good hack. And think vertically — wall space is an untapped resource in many homes!

Keep It Clean ✦ 105

Get the Light Right

The light in your home impacts everything.

From the potential use of a space to the way colours and patterns appear in your home — natural lighting is key. If you are starting from scratch with a renovation or extension then you are lucky enough to be able to factor in how to get the most natural light into your home from the get-go, but realistically most of us are just trying to make the best of what we have.

Making the Most of Dark Corners

There will always be some rooms in our homes that are more naturally blessed with good light, such as south-facing ones. For rooms that are gloomier, you have two options: first choice, don't fight it. Lean into it and embrace the dark side, go for a cosy, snuggly space. Obviously, that might not work for every room lacking in light, for instance a deep forest-green drenched room might not be everyone's ideal nursery. In this case, you need to explore options to let light in. Are there doors that can have glass panels rather than wood? This is a great way to borrow natural light. Another good idea is to check that your furniture isn't blocking light or casting shadows. If so, try rearranging your furniture to find out if there is a configuration that brightens the room. My favourite tip, which works really well for small and dark spaces, is the addition of a mirror: it will reflect light around the room. The fact there are so many quirky shaped or fabulous vintage mirrors to shop from definitely doesn't make this a chore.

Once you have analysed the light in your rooms, you can use this information to influence your design choices. As I've previously said, I am not one for rules, however there is no denying that light can change the appearance of a space, so it is prudent to take this into consideration. If ever there was a reason for testing your paints before diving in, this is it. A colour can appear an entirely different hue when in a north-facing room with a cold light in comparison to how it looks in its warm southern counterpart. Light won't just change the way paints appear, but also your soft furnishings, textiles and patterns; so, along with your paints, it's well worth testing out swatches, and anything else you can lay your hands on, before making your final design choices.

Get in the Zone

Just as we might use paint to create zones in our homes, we can use lighting in a similar way. This is particularly useful in open-plan living. In these spaces you will want low-level, ambient lighting so you can relax, but as these spaces are often multi-functional you will also need alternative lights in the areas where you might also be doing work, study or reading. In these zones you could add lamps as 'task lighting'. The same approach can be taken in the dining area, so that when you are entertaining you can highlight this space.

Mood Lighting

As anyone with seasonal affective disorder (SAD) will know, as humans we crave the light. There is nothing more natural than the sun rising and setting, and our bodies are prompted by light to regulate our systems and release hormones.

Just as our bodies need light, they also need the dark for periods of rest, so it is important to make sure you are creating a home environment that assists your body with this natural rhythm. This is particularly important in the bedroom; you won't want to have bright cold-toned lights, it's better to go for those with warmer, red undertones, which will make you feel relaxed in the lead up to bedtime and aid in the production of melatonin to help you feel well rested.

And, of course, I can't close this section without a mention of the humble candle. Or not so humble now that you can get them in every shape and size possible, from a Rubenesque bust to a piece of fruit. Obviously, these particular works of art are not for burning, but there is something so special about the warm glow from the ones that are. The nostalgic and romantic cosiness of a flickering flame is something I believe wholeheartedly can instantly improve your mood.

Get the Light Right ✦ 109

Big Light vs Little Light

The right lighting is essential in creating the desired mood in your home, so let's get straight down to the hot debate: Are you team big light or small light!?

There is, of course, a time and place for both, but following on from a viral TikTok debate, it seems that the majority of the Internet is team small light. It isn't surprising with the sheer variety of quirky, cool smaller lights and lamps that are available, and can be used to create a far cosier vibe than the sometimes stark and clinical big light. It's also incredibly easy to upcycle lamps and lampshades, which means that you can add to your collection and switch things up easily.

Don't get me wrong though, I love a big statement lampshade in the centre of the room – such as a coloured glass chandelier, a mid-century pendant, or even something wild and feathered – and especially when it's popping against a beautifully painted ceiling. But I'm a firm believer that most spaces benefit from at least one lamp, too. In fact, there are so many incredible options out there, that add way more to your home than simply a source to see by; so, I say the more the merrier!

And with the emergence of the battery bulb, you don't even need to be limited by plug sockets anymore! Layering your light sources with a variety of lamps and the overhead light, means you have enough options for every eventuality.

I am not really a fan of spotlights, probably as, by nature, I choose pretty over practical every time, but I recognize the need for them in some places. I reached the compromise in my kitchen of having an overhead light, so that I can tick the pretty box, combined with spotlights over the counter as, according to Jon, we need to see when we cook...seems OTT if you ask me?! With the popularity of kitchen islands there has been a rise in beautiful pendants that fit perfectly into your kitchen design and mean you don't need to sacrifice aesthetics for function.

Get the Light Right

Plan, Plan, Plan

As you might have noticed, I keep harping on about trialling, testing and planning.

Trust me, I have learned the hard way how essential it is to have a plan. I am a textbook creative who just dives in and lives to regret it. I probably have mild PTSD from the stress of failed projects and, as a result, have gone completely the other way — I am now one of those people who has endless lists.

Keeping a written plan, along with a daily and weekly task list on a calendar, is something that really helps me and keeps me on track. You can buy specific DIY planners...and who doesn't love a pretty notebook? For those more tech savvy than me, Excel is the perfect tool for project management.

So, what to put into that planner? That's the million-dollar question. First, you will need to think about what you are trying to achieve. If you are juggling multiple projects, I recommend keeping a separate plan for each one to keep it clear and simple. It's also worth considering your future plans for the house as a whole at this point. If you are planning to repurpose a room but know that it is a temporary measure as in the next couple of years you will be extending, you probably don't want to spend loads of money. So, think Ikea-hack storage rather than bespoke dream cupboards.

Once you know what your end goal is then you can start your research. It's important to know exactly what you will need to do to complete the project. At this stage you can decide if you, or anyone you live with, is up to the job or if you will be hiring in. If you think you are capable and willing to do the work, it's worth watching some tutorials and doing your research properly if it's something you haven't tried before. Once you know the tasks you need to complete, break them down into subtasks and delegate responsibility for their completion, be it to a tradesperson or to your other half. Knowing who is accountable is important so nothing slips through a gap.

❖ The Core Principles of Dopamine Decor

Be Realistic About Budget

You will need to budget for:

- Materials, for instance timber, nails, paint, etc.
- For the purchase or hire of tools
- Potentially for the hire of a tradesperson for some or all of the work, depending on your skillset and time availability

Of course, like so many of us, I am always looking for ways to keep costs down. That could be finding cheap materials on local Facebook groups or eBay, buying in bulk, opting to try out an IKEA hack rather than buy something bespoke, or repurposing what you already have.

I always give myself leeway as projects often go over budget, it's not unheard of for me to stay on track, but it's a pleasant surprise.

Factor in Time

Everything always takes longer than you think, so give yourself a realistic amount of time to complete a project. I take full responsibility for being a part of this social-media culture where we tap a paint brush and the room is transformed. In reality, it takes many hours of preparation and hard work to achieve those results.

Most of us are also living busy lives on top of carrying out DIY projects. We are squeezing in renos or room makeovers around families and work, so it is important to set a realistic timeline. If you don't, you will either end up rushing the job and not being happy with the results, or adding pressure to an already stressful situation. As someone prone to trying to complete too many projects at once, I have learned that allowing yourself extra time and managing your expectations is key to a smooth-running project.

Also, it's beneficial to remember that even with the best planning in the world, sometimes things still don't work out. Be it something out of your control, or that you just don't like something you had chosen, it's OK to feel disappointed but we are all human and make mistakes. Just brush yourself off, get a new sheet on that planner and start again!

PART TWO:

THE DOPAMINE HOME, ROOM BY ROOM

Living Room

The living room is a very well-used space and forms the centre of the home, so you want to make design choices that mean it's somewhere that you truly want to be.

As the name suggests, this is the room most of us end up *living* in, whatever that looks like to you. From family Netflix marathons to girly pamper evenings or cosy scrabble sessions, above all else you want your living room to be relaxing and a place you relish coming home to. There is no better feeling than curating a space unique to you, in which you are surrounded by things that delight you, and the living room, where you will spend so much of your time, is the prime space for this.

Take a Seat

Seating is probably the most important design choice you will make in the living room — this is a room to unwind in, so comfort is key. Your decisions in this area will be led by the size of the room you are working with: we have a configuration of two small sofas as our living room is on the smaller side, but there is a whole world of giant, squashy corner sofas, statement chairs or love seats to suit all room shapes and sizes. Not only is your seating somewhere to collapse after a hard day or to cuddle up with your loved ones (furry or human!), but seating can also provide a beautiful focal point with a pop of colour or pattern.

Keep it Clutter Free

Keeping the living space as organized as possible will help to make the most of your space and keep stress levels over clutter and mess at bay. As a family with young children, we have spent the last few years in the 'toys everywhere' stage. Luckily, as the kids get older, the toys get smaller, and there are now no noisy plastic monstrosities killing my carefully curated vibe. Of course, if you have a young family there will always be the 'clutter' of toys, books and games; finding a way to keep most of this stored out of sight is key to creating a relaxed space that adults can enjoy as well as children.

There are so many great storage solutions that work perfectly in living rooms, such as sexy sideboards, fitted alcove cabinets or shelves, and vintage drinks cabinets, to name a few. Remember, this is a space you want to feel relaxed and comfortable in, so make sure you set it up with a quick clean-up in mind, for those evenings when you just need to sweep everything into its designated drawer and then collapse in front of the television.

Speaking of which...as well as seating and storage, another essential in most living rooms is the television. Although the pretty pictures on Pinterest and Instagram would have you believe that no one owns a TV, we all know that it is a fairly central feature in most households. However, you don't need to accept the TV as an eyesore; instead, turn it into a feature that brings you pleasure. If your budget stretches to it, you can get a fancy frame TV; if not, you can make your own fun surround or find a way to incorporate it into a colourful gallery wall.

The living room should be your personal sanctuary from the chaos of the outside world, somewhere you can feel at peace and recharge your batteries. It is your own haven, so be led in your design decisions by decor that makes you feel relaxed and happy. If you do that, you can't go wrong.

Make the Fireplace a Feature

When we bought our home, it came complete with an electric fire in the living room. Despite it being dated — sadly not in a cool, retro way — we seized the potential and decided that, just because we had bought an ex-council house with zero character, why couldn't we imitate a classy period home? We ripped out the original electric fire and added a fire surround and mantle that we had found on eBay, and we have never looked back.

    A fireplace is not only a celebrated feature, providing warmth and character to a room, but it also offers endless styling potential. My mantel has been dressed for every season, and you don't have to go all out. Sometimes adding a plant and some colourful candles is all you need to elevate the room and inject some personality. If a more traditional fireplace isn't your style, you could opt for a log burner; there are so many options, including some incredible colourful ones, which definitely provide the wow factor.

Shoestring Tip

Reuse and upcycle your fire surround. Facebook Marketplace, eBay, Freecycle, or your local reuse centre, are all great places to find an old fire surround and mantel. I have even spotted ones on street pavements outside a reno! They are simple to fit yourself, and with a lick of paint you will have created your very own fireplace to cosy up to.

A showstopper fireplace and logburner – Carla Elliman (@carlaelliman)

The Dopamine Home, Room by Room

Your Coffee Table is a Focal Point

A coffee table is a great way to add a statement to your living space. Not only can you select a table that itself is a gorgeous focal point, but you can also style it with your favourite pieces — think bold, beautiful books stacked up, quirky candles and a fun vase. As we are short on space in my home, I chose an acrylic table as the transparency gives the illusion of more space. I also selected it for its shape: it has a showstopper wavy base that casts little rainbows around the room when the sun hits, lifting my soul instantly.

My three top tips for choosing your coffee table:

1. **Size:** Go for a coffee table the same height as your sofa and two-thirds the length

2. **Practicality:** Choose a piece suited to your situation — you won't want something with sharp corners or made of glass if you have small people running around

3. **Styling**: 'Shop' your home and switch things up frequently to keep your look fresh, you don't need to buy new bits to style your coffee table

Living Room • 125

Combine Comfort and Beauty

For someone as notorious as Henry VIII for falling out of love with things, my beautiful burnt-orange velvet sofa has stood the test of time where many have not. I'm not even ashamed to admit that the children are often forbidden from sitting on it, so fearful am I of its ruin.

The reason this sofa is so very perfect is that it is both comfortable and beautiful, an extremely rare find. When buying sofas there is so much to consider: Will it fit the space? Is it comfy? How many do we need? How can we make sure it's in the prime spot to watch the TV? This means that sometimes the aesthetics get forgotten, which is sad as the sofa is such a great opportunity to add colour and pattern to your home.

Our two sofas are pink and orange – one of my favourite joy-inducing colour combinations – but you can get them in virtually any design, from green to yellow to leopard print. And if you can't find a ready-made model that makes you happy, you can upcycle or reupholster one to make your very own sofa of dreams.

Express Yourself With Art

There is no better way to lift your spirits than to be surrounded by artwork that brings you happiness simply by being in its vicinity. Including prints and art in your living room is a great way to add pops of colour and pattern. Art no longer needs to be expensive, there are plenty of affordable and accessible options for both prints and frames. I personally love to pick up vintage frames second hand. What you want to achieve in your home is to be surrounded by an environment that makes you feel joyous, and if that's seeing your child's first drawing, a napkin that your partner doodled on during a special date, or a scrap of material from a loved dress, you can find a way to incorporate this into your art too, don't be held back by traditions.

How to Curate and Hang a Gallery Wall

A gallery wall full of your favourite prints and collections is never going to fail to make you smile. Here is my guide to creating a cohesive gallery wall easily. Remember, as with 99 per cent of DIY, **planning is key!**

You Will Need

Art/ prints/ interesting objects

Frames

Drill

Rawlplugs, screws and hooks (alternatively, use picture-hanging strips)

Level

1. Choose your artworks/prints:
If you are buying specifically for a brand-new gallery wall, rather than shopping your home, it's a great idea to take to Pinterest for inspo, or to create a moodboard for how you would like the gallery wall to look.

COLOUR When choosing your art consider the background. If the gallery wall is going onto a bold coloured wall or wallpaper, make sure the prints you select are in the right tones. A fun colour clash can look amazing, but it's worth checking the contrast tickles your fancy as some colour combinations can be over- or underwhelming.

Also consider the colours in each piece in relation to one another. There are no rules, but my guidance would be to select pieces with a theme. That could be a theme in the subject, flowers for instance, or colour cohesion, so perhaps one small accent of colour running through all the prints.

SCALE I feel the most beautifully curated gallery walls are those that use art in different sizes. The contrast adds instant interest and dimension.

2. **Collect your frames:** Gather all the frames you will be using for the artwork — these may be newly purchased, second-hand finds, or shopping your home. The main decision will be if you want to go for matching frames or a variety.

   MATCHING When I curate a gallery wall, if there isn't a clear theme running through the art, then I use matching frames (all white or gold, for instance) to create a harmonious look.

   VARIETY If the art is already corresponding in pattern, colour or design, a mish-mash of frames works really nicely as there is already unity in the prints. This is actually my favourite look as it is less flat.

3. **Gather your 'extras':** This could be neon signs, wall-mounted planters or vases, decorative birds — whatever makes you happy! And, of course, if you don't want extras, skip this step!

Living Room

4. Test the layout: Once your art is in the chosen frames, arrange your pieces into a layout to check which look best next to each other. You want to make sure your gallery wall is balanced, so you don't want all the large prints next to each other. A good way to test the layout is to map it out on the floor to get the general idea first, and then to decide where they should go on the wall.

To decide the wall placement, trace your frames onto paper, then cut each shape out and stick them temporarily onto the wall. This stage will probably involve a lot of moving things around and repositioning.

In her book, *Mad About the House*, Kate Watson-Smyth recommends hanging art so 'the centre of the piece is roughly at eye level'. Obviously, that isn't possible for a gallery wall, so my guidance would be for the centre point of the total arrangement to be at eye level.

The spacing between your prints is down to your personal taste. I like my pieces to sit quite close to one another, and that also works well if you have a small space to work with as you can fit more pieces in, but there is no hard-and-fast rule.

When setting out your gallery wall, don't forget to mix in your 'extras' at regular intervals. Having a few horizontal pieces looks great, too (see the diagram on page 129).

If you struggle to find the right configuration for your prints, there are lots of gallery wall templates available online.

5. Time to put them up!
Don't forget that a gallery wall doesn't have to be permanent. If you don't want to, or can't, drill lots of holes into your walls then picture-hanging strips and hooks are your friends.

Paint Your Radiator

Unless you have underfloor heating, radiators are a typical feature of most rooms. Bring them into your design by painting them perfectly. I like to blend my rads in with my walls, but you could make yours a fun contrasting colour if you fancy something more fun!

You Will Need

Dust sheet

Masking tape

Sugar soap and cloth

120-grit sandpaper

Primer (optional)

Paint of your choice

Paint brush or small roller

> Most importantly, make sure you can do this at a time when you can switch the heating off for twenty-four hours.

1. **Prep:** Switch the heating off, put down a dust sheet to protect the floor and tape up any areas, such as valves, that you don't want to paint.

2. **Clean:** Give your radiator a really good clean, no one wants all those dust bunnies getting painted over and etched forever into your lovely new colourful radiator!

3. **Sand and prime:** According to Rust-oleum 'bare metal surfaces need to be primed with a suitable metal primer, whereas previously painted surfaces (or the factory finish) should be abraded and degreased'. So, either sand and degrease with sugar soap, or sand and prime, as required.

   When sanding, use 120-grit sandpaper and make sure to get into all the groves.

   My go-to primer is Zinsser, but most paint brands have their own primer for metal too.

4. **Paint:** You can use a specialist radiator paint, paint that's suitable for metal, or I have often just used good-quality emulsion and it has stood the test of time.

    You can apply paint with a brush or roller, both are effective. It will usually need two to three coats. Remember to leave your heating off for twenty-four hours while the paint dries to avoid any bubbling.

What Lies Beneath

Painting behind a radiator can be a faff, but with a combination of a long-handled roller and brush, you should be able to achieve the angle to paint all those hard-to-reach patches. Alternatively, there are some fab little tools that have started popping up on the market: they have a long, flat paint pad on an extendable handle, which can slide behind the radiator, leaving the perfect finish. You can also use them in other awkward-to-paint spots, such as behind cabinets or utilities, so well worth adding one to your decorating kit!

The most joyous kitchen diner – Laura Hall (@thehexagonalhouse)

Kitchen

For someone who can't cook, I am strangely drawn to kitchens!

There is just something so exciting about all those gleaming gadgets, the snazzy little storage solutions and the endless options for cabinets, shelves and — that holy grail of kitchen features — the much-coveted pantry.

To my mind, the living room is the heart of the home, but perhaps the more culinary inclined would argue that this accolade belongs to the kitchen. Food, and the preparation of it, is a way to bring those you love together, and central to socializing and celebrating. We no longer have kitchens that are only entered to cook in, the emergence of the kitchen-diner has seen kitchens become multi-functional spaces used for food preparation, eating and socializing — everyone knows the kitchen is where the best bits of a party happen!

The very best of bold and bright kitchens – Carla Elliman (@carlaelliman)

As with all the rooms in your home, you will want to make the space work for *you* based on what makes *you* tick. If you see your kitchen as more of a place to have nibbles and drinks, rather than preparing gastronomical delights, then perhaps you will prioritize bougie wine coolers or creating a cool coffee corner over an expensive combi oven. This is your home, so make your decor choices based on what makes you happy and how you want the space to work for you, rather than on the 'norm' or some mythical future buyer.

Turn the Colour Up

Gone are the days of neutral-only kitchens, there are so many amazing colourful options out there now, you can buy kitchens in maroon, pastel pink, olive green and everything between. And if your kitchen isn't to your taste but you can't afford a full refit, or perhaps you rent, don't fear! There are lots of ways to refresh existing cabinetry using paint or vinyl wraps, which are more affordable and easily reversed. You can also add colour and pattern to existing units with paint, wallpaper and art. Or bring a pop of colour into the room through your appliances: from kettles to toasters, the stalwart kitchen gadgets now come in a range of vibrant colours. I'm greeted in the morning by the happiest sunshine-yellow coffee machine, which gives me that extra boost alongside my daily caffeine kick. And, again, it doesn't have to be a new purchase: if your existing appliances are on the boring side, you can always keep them cute with a lick of paint or decorative wrap.

Flooring is another way to bring character into your kitchen. I am a huge fan of tiles, due to the sheer number of pretty patterns out there, again, in an amazing range of colours. There are also less permanent options such as stick-on tiles or adding LVT or lino. I also love a stencilled tile, if the ones you have inherited are a little bland. A little imaginative thinking can go a long way towards creating your dream dopamine kitchen.

The key to a happy kitchen is to fill it with personality and tailor it to your needs. Whereas the living room is somewhere to relax and kick back, the kitchen is a livelier space: it's about bringing people together, celebrating food and drink, having a chat over a cuppa, and making memories.

Cutest shelfie – Poppy Pearson (@letsgotopoppys)

Put on a Display

Open shelves are no longer the new kid on the block, but there is no sign of our love for this marvellous hybrid of styling and storage slowing down. The styling potential of open shelves is unmatched. Got a kitchen that is missing a pop of colour or personality? Then open shelves are your quick-and-easy way to address this.

We made shelving out of scaffold boards, which provides the feel-good factor of repurposing something, but there are plenty of other options if rustic isn't your style, from sleek marble to industrial steel. The real beauty of open shelving is that, while a practical storage solution, the styling opportunities are endless. For someone like me, who tires of their surroundings quickly, changing the decor you have on display is the perfect way to switch the look of a room easily, and with zero cost.

Kitchen ◆ 139

Simple Shelf-styling Tips

Follow these tips and creating an eye-catching display of things that make your heart happy will be super simple.

1. **Collect together everything that you want to display.** Choose objects that are a range of sizes: you will want some with height, and I love to include dangly plants to add an extra dimension. It can be helpful to have an accent colour or theme running through the objects.

2. **Find an item to use as the central focus.** I work from the centre out when I plan my shelves and aim for a loose triangle shape. I would usually pick something taller, like a statement vase or a print, to be the central point and then work my way out with smaller items.

3. **Art looks great on a shelf.** Overlapped prints can look modern and edgy, or a bold larger piece is great to sit in a central spot.

4. **Arrange items in groups of odd numbers.** To create a balanced look, keep your number of items to an odd number – that is, three, five or seven. Odd numbers create a more aesthetically pleasing look. Don't fill every space, or the items will become lost.

5. **Add seasonal touches.** Flowers or fairy lights will make the display a real showstopper.

Go Bold With Your Appliances

Growing up I only saw white washing machines and dryers, something that makes no sense to me as doing the laundry is already so dreary. Surely a pink washer would make the chores less painful? Luckily, things have improved and there are some seriously sexy metallic numbers out there now. However, in comparison to the cool colourful fridges you can buy (thank you Smeg), they are still lacking. Step forward the DIY community who have been taking this matter into their own hands with prettily painted appliances cropping up all over Instagram. Our washing machine and dishwasher have been painted a light green for two years now, and the difference a lick of paint has made is phenomenal. When I used to walk into the kitchen, all I could see were the ugly appliances, now they blend in with my colour palette flawlessly. I don't think I will ever have white appliances again!

Colourful appliances inject fun into a kitchen, such as my sunshine yellow coffee machine and, opposite, Helen Ford's baby blue numbers (@homewithhelenandco).

How to Paint Your Washing Machine

Say goodbye to eyesore appliances easily with a lick of paint. I have painted my washing machine and dishwasher using the method below, but you could zhuzh up the fridge-freezer, tumble dryer or any appliance you fancy! Your kitchen will be transformed into an uninterrupted thing of beauty, you can thank me later.

You Will Need

Dust sheet

Masking tape

Sugar soap

180-grit sandpaper

Primer suitable for metal (do not use a water-based product)

Paint suitable for metal

Small foam paint roller and tray

Paint brush

Varnish (either indoor or outdoor variety is fine, just be sure it's clear drying)

1. **Prep:** Switch the appliance off at the socket, put down a dust sheet and tape up any buttons etc., that you don't want to paint.

2. **Clean:** Give your appliance a really good clean, sugar soap is best.

3. **Sand:** Give the appliance a very light sand to help the paint adhere.

4. **Prime:** Zinsser primer is my preferred choice, but you can use any primer suitable for metal. Do not use a water-based primer. Apply according to the instructions on the tin.

5. **Apply paint:** Metal paint or all-surface paint is ideal for this job, apply at least two coats using a roller for a smooth finish.

6. **Leave to dry for twenty-four hours,** with the appliance still switched off.

7. **Seal:** Paint with two coats of clear indoor or outdoor varnish. Do not use the appliance for twenty-four hours after application.

The Dopamine Home, Room by Room

Set Up Your Own Coffee Corner

Since lockdown everyone's a barista, right? What started as a fad, with us all learning to make our own iced vanilla lattes, has blossomed into a permanent obsession in our homes. And it's not just coffee, we are embracing matcha, bubble tea and all sorts of other fancy beverages. We spend so much time in our homes, so why not properly enjoy it!? Of course, we also want an array of cute mugs, jugs and jars to complement our fancy new equipment. Enter, the coffee bar.

Having a coffee bar is a really fun addition if you have space in your kitchen and a trend that I am very much here for...even I can manage to brew up a coffee!

Make the Most of Your Space With an Island

As I'm never going to have my own tropical island, I have set my heart on having one of the kitchen variety in my next home. Kitchen islands are designed in so many different shapes and styles, that — unless you are restricted by space (like me) — there really is something for everyone. As with all the areas in your home, you want to consider how you spend your time in that space and what makes you happy, and capitalize on that. If you love cooking, you might want to design an island with loads of space to prep and the hob and oven in the centre, so you can cook while chatting with friends and family. Or, if you want it to be more of a social spot for friends to drink wine or kids to do their homework, then you might prefer a simple breakfast bar with some stylish statement stools for everyone to pull up a seat.

The kitchen island of dreams — Sophia Ferrari-Wills (@thiscolourfulnest)

Dining Room

Long gone are the days when a dining room was a place devoted solely to sitting and eating.

It's now a place to sit and eat, to do the kids' homework and, quite possibly, a work-from-home station, too. The traditional dining room, a space designed purely to dine and entertain, is something of a luxury nowadays. Many of us struggle for space and have to use rooms in a multi-functional way, but that needn't mean sacrificing style. With considered choices, it's still possible to design a hybrid, functional dining room packed with joy-inducing character.

150 ❖ The Dopamine Home, Room by Room

Think Function

A great starting point when planning a dining room is to reflect on how you will be using this space and what your priorities are. There is no point curating a grand entertaining space when, in reality, the only thing you will be hosting are Zoom meetings from your dining table, with your WFH microwave meal to accompany you. Write a list of all the ways in which you and your family, or housemates, use the space, and roughly order them in rank of importance — that is, the thing you use the room most for should go at the top of your list.

Once you have considered how you will really be using your dining room (or 'dining area' if you have an open-plan living space) on a day-to-day basis, then you can start to think about how to make sure the space is flexible to meet all those needs. Choose lighting that is interchangeable, such as lamps and dimmers, making the segue between cocktail parties and study sessions seamless. Selecting storage carefully is key — you could incorporate floor-to-ceiling bookshelves, which appear beautiful while simultaneously organizing everything you need for work and school; or, for a cleaner look, opt for cleverly disguised floor-to-ceiling cupboards that meld into the room. Also, think wisely about your central piece: your dining table.

You won't want something huge if your space is small or you are just a couple (unless you are those fun hosts that I wish I was).

Inject the Fun!

Of course, designing your dream dining room won't all be practical considerations, you can still go wild with colours, textures and patterns. Continue to weave the threads of your favourite palettes through this space. I have a small dining room, but it hasn't held me back from embracing a pink ceiling, bold botanical wallpaper and an assortment of rugs that change nearly as often as I change my socks! A dining room is a space that lends itself naturally to fun interiors, after all, the original focus is entertaining, what's not to love? So, my advice would be: don't hold back, create a room — or corner — that is a pocketful of joy.

Upcycle a Cocktail Cabinet

When I spotted this charity-shop find, I knew it had potential to be my new cocktail cabinet. I just needed that piney-orange gone and some small modifications to give this unloved piece a fresh new look. These are the steps I took for this specific upcycle, but you can apply the fundamentals to your own thrifted finds.

You Will Need

- Dust sheet
- Sugar soap
- Masking tape
- 120-grit sandpaper
- Wood filler
- Primer (if your paint doesn't have an in-built primer, most furniture paints do)
- Paint (furniture paint or suitable for wood, ideally)
- Paint brush
- Small paint roller
- Paint tray
- Wallpaper
- Wallpaper adhesive
- Wallpaper brush
- Wallpaper roller
- Drill
- Screws
- Screwdriver
- New hardwear (handles, pulls, etc.)
- Legs (optional)
- Lights (optional)

1. **Clean:** Lay down a dust sheet and thoroughly clean the cabinet. This will give you a chance to assess the condition and identify any areas that need repair. I use sugar soap for this.

2. **Remove any parts of the cabinet you no longer need or want:** I didn't like the base of the cabinet as it gave the piece a boxy shape. So, I removed this using a chisel and hammer. I also removed the old door handles and the broken lights.

3. **Fill and sand:** Fill any holes left by the handles and lights with wood filler, and sand to smooth once dry.

4. **Screw on new legs:** Changing the shape of your piece and lifting a cabinet off the ground by adding new legs, is the easiest way to improve the appearance.

5. **Key the cabinet:** To do this, you simply sand the wood lightly so the paint adheres well.

6. **Prep for paint:** Tape up any areas you don't want paint on — around the glass, for instance.

7. **Prime:** You may not need to do this if you are using furniture paint as many have the primer built in. However, if you are painting onto a tricky substrate, such as melamine, a primer will still be beneficial.

8. **Paint the cabinet:** Using a small roller will give the best finish, rather than a brush, which will leave strokes.

9. **Wallpaper the back panel:** I use wallpaper paste for this as it makes it easy to work with the paper to match the pattern, but you can use PVA or spray adhesive, if you prefer. Smooth out any bubbles with a wallpaper brush and go over joins with a roller to give a seamless finish.

10. **Add lights:** Install peel-and-stick battery-powered lights in place of any old, broken electronics.

11. **Replace handles:** Drill new holes if necessary, and fit your handles of choice.

Dining Room ❋ 153

Bartender!

A really special addition to a dining room is a cocktail cabinet or drinks trolley, and it's not just for those who enjoy a tipple! They are the perfect place to display your treasures: my cabinet shows off pretty plates, bowls and vases, and you can stock yours with whatever brings you joy. I get such satisfaction thrifting an unloved cabinet on Facebook Marketplace, or in a second-hand store, and giving it a whole new look. Paint is an obvious choice for this, but I also love experimenting with adding wallpaper, vinyl, gold leaf and, of course, some new hardware, such as handles, drawer pulls or knobs. You can really go all out with a cocktail cabinet; they are supposed to be decadent and dramatic, so go wild!

Design With Storage in Mind

We have a really cute wood and cane sideboard in our dining room that is great for stashing our plethora of board games and my obscene number of vases. A sideboard is a lovely storage option as they are so pretty, and I love that you can style the top with plants, vases and prints.

If you are fortunate enough to be able to add fitted storage, it is a fantastic use of space. Floor-to-ceiling storage always looks incredibly classy, and you can hide away all the clutter that can pile up and leave you feeling unsettled. Fitted units are particularly great for tidying away any unsightly work or school-related bits that you might also be using in your dining space.

Get the Dining Table Right

The table should be your first consideration when furnishing your dining room: it is your centrepiece, so you want to get it right.

    We opted for a round table because our dining room is very small. A circular or square table in a compact space will give you more free space. Another great space saver are tables with benches, as you can tuck the benches under the table when not in use. Banquettes, which can line the corner of the room, are another excellent way to get the most of your space; and, if you are really pushed for space, an extendable table is a great idea.

    If you are not limited by space, there are masses of fantastic oval and rectangle shapes that are made to fill a gorgeous large area. As with all your room planning, you want to make sure you balance these sensible considerations with listening to your gut about what will make you feel happy and at peace in your home.

Whether open-plan or a separate dining room, the table is the focal point — Ellie Lawrence (@sevenpalmtreehouse)

Dining Room

A bold rug makes a statement in a sumptuous dining room — Joanne Hardcastle (@hardcastletowers)

Make the Most of the Floor

In a dining room you want a floor that you can easily clean in the likely event of food spillages, but that doesn't mean you need to limit yourself to soulless bland flooring. There is a dazzling range of gorgeous washable rugs out there; I have tested a lot of them so you don't have to, and I can confirm that they do exactly what it says on the tin. So, don't be afraid to have an incredible burst of joyous pattern and colour in the shape of a rug in your dining room. Your dining room should be warm and inviting, and a rug will go a long way towards creating that welcoming environment.

Hallway

Your hallway is your home's chance to make a great first impression; it is the space that sets the tone for the rest of your interior.

When designing this space, think about how your visitors will *feel* when they step inside — and, just as importantly, how the space will make *you* feel on your return home after a day of work, trip away or quick dash to the shops.

First stop: how does the space work currently? Are you greeted by an ever-growing pile of shoes, rivalling even Mount Everest's slopes, and accessorized by an impressive balancing act of coat Jenga on your banister? If so, it might be time to rethink your hallway design.

Second: how do you *want* the space to work and feel? Your goal should be to be welcomed with an immediate feel-good factor when you enter your home. So, depending on what brings you joy, try and include some of that to greet you and your guests. For instance, when I step inside my front door, I'm met by a pop of pink banister decorated with faux greenery. It is a sight that never fails to lift my spirits, particularly at Christmas when it is festooned with baubles, too.

The Challenges of Hallways

You want your hallway to give a tantalizing taste of your home aesthetic, but this area is not without its challenges. If your hallway is constantly being clogged up with trip hazards, such the kids' muddy football boots, a pram or your workout gear, then you are fighting a losing battle to maintain the feel-good factor you crave when entering your home after a long day. Your hallway will be a high-traffic area, so you need to bear your lifestyle in mind when you are designing this space. Make sure you include clever, often multi-functional, storage that will work hard to make this space clutter free and give you and your guests the welcome you deserve.

Disorder isn't the only common complaint in hallway design; size and shape are also often problematic. It's likely your hallway is narrow and lacking in light, but don't lose hope! There are many tricks to address this, such as the colour palette you decorate in, using the best lighting options and artful use of mirrors — the way they can make a space look larger is nothing short of sorcery!

Set the Tone

Your hallway is the trailer to the movie of your home, so make sure it reels people in. Anyone entering your home will immediately catch a glimpse into the themes and colours that are the foundation of your style. In my home, guests can instantly see the pinks and greens that underpin and flow throughout; they know within the first few paces that in my home, we have a love of plants and botanical wallpapers. Your hallway is so much more than a means to get to the next room, so don't neglect it. This is the perfect area to weave together all the threads of your home into one cohesive, beautiful space.

Flowing through the home, a perfect peek of pastel – Helen Ford (@homewithhelenandco)

Hallway • 163

A Place for Everything

Now, back to the shoe mountains and coat Jenga. Your hallway is most likely a smallish space, unless you are fortunate enough to have a grand entrance hall, so you need to design the space to work for you on a practical level and make sure there is a place to keep everything. Don't forget: the less clutter, the happier you will feel. So, balancing pretty with practical is a win-win situation.

If you are lucky enough to have a boot room or porch to keep most of the 'clutter', you will probably still want an element of storage in the entrance hallway for all those odds-and-ends we plonk down as we come through the front door, such as keys and change. But in this case, you can go for a small storage option. We have a little upcycled cabinet with a tray for keys and drawers for seasonal extras, such as scarves and sun cream, which works perfectly for all the small items that seem to gather!

The warmest welcome to a vibrant home – Hannah Clark (@little_edwardian_semi)

Perfect painting creates a sensational staircase – Charlotte Cannon (@homeofcharl)

Don't Neglect the Stairs

Your stairs are another place in your home where it can be easily forgotten that you can still stamp your personality. Yes, they are there to get from A to B, but who's to say you can't get from A to B while looking at perfectly placed gallery walls, stunning art and pretty panelling? Long gone are the days where everyone's stairs were carpeted in beige. We are now seeing all manner of gorgeous statement staircases, from luxurious leopard-print deep pile to gold leaf and rainbow painted. Why not give your staircase the wow factor that makes it a joy to climb, or at the very least less of a chore!

My Top Three Tips for Painting Stairs

Stairs and banisters are notoriously tricky to paint so here are my three top tips to take the stress out of your staircase makeover.

1. **Plan carefully:** This is key. You want to pick a time when there are minimal people moving around; so, perhaps bedtime if you have children, or when no one is home that day. Most importantly, plan the direction you are painting (up or down) and make sure that once you paint the last step you will be finishing on the floor where you need to be. The last thing you need is to be stranded upstairs when you are supposed to be out of the house for school pick up or a meeting!

2. **Sand:** No matter how tempting it might be to go straight over old paint or unprepared wood, you will get a better finish when you sand first. Using 120-grit sandpaper, go over the steps to remove any old paint and also to create a key for your paint to adhere to.

3. **The sock hack:** This is an easy technique to enable speedy and even paint coverage around all the nooks and crannies of tricky-to-paint spindles. Layer a plastic glove and a sock on your hand like a mitt, dip the sock (while wearing it) into the paint tub and then rub the banister until it's covered. So simple, and strangely satisfying too!

Make Use of Dead Space

I have seen some genius uses of understair spaces, everything from natty storage to clever mini office nooks. Even if you are using yours in a more traditional 'dump all the bags-for-life and cleaning products' fashion, there is no reason that you can't make it look attractive at the same time. You can wallpaper the outside as well as the interior, and make the cupboard door pop with a cute paint job and updated handle. Life really is too short to keep your doors factory-setting white.

Choose Your Colours Wisely

When we originally decorated our hallway, we went for a dark teal paint. The rationale behind this was partly to embrace the small size of the corridor, in the hope that it would appear elegant and considered, and partly to make the rooms leading off the hall feel larger in comparison. Unfortunately, the effect was just plain old claustrophobic (though admittedly the dark paint did cover all manner of sins, such as small sticky handprints).

Having said that, a beautiful dark hallway can work well in larger spaces, especially those with high ceilings. Since redecorating, we have gone for a two-tone pink and green that carries down the stairs and through the hallway. It is the same green that is on the appliances in the kitchen, which you can see directly at the end of the hall, and the continuous flow of the colours helps to give a feeling of space and connection throughout the house.

Let in the Light

Hallways are often small and lacking in natural light, so choosing the right lighting is important (see page 107–111). In our hall, we opted for a pretty glass pendant that is similar to the one in the adjacent kitchen, to help with the continuity in the decor. If we had a higher ceiling, or we didn't have a six-foot Jon, an incredible statement pendant or chandelier always looks fantastic in the entrance to a hallway. As the hall is normally a space with less furnishings, lighting has the chance to stand out, so making a bold choice will really pay off.

And the flawless hallway styling is carried on to the upstairs landing – Charlotte Cannon (@homeofcharl)

Bathroom

Just because the bathroom is a functional room, it doesn't mean it needs to lack personality.

I love our bathroom. The decorative floor tiles paired with the dark, dramatic forest wallpaper and the plant-laden shelves are just the right amount of pattern, colour and botany to fill my cup. However, as much as I adore the aesthetics and the way this space brings me happiness, I would redesign the layout in a flash.

When we moved in, we had small children and the daily ritual of bathing them was one of life's great pleasures. Now we are all older, dashing around like headless chickens in pre-bedtime pandemonium, and a shower is the smart choice. In a tiny bathroom like ours, all the now unused bath space seems a waste, and I dream of a beautifully tiled, huge walk-in shower.

Look at Your Layout

If you are starting out fresh, make sure you not only consider aesthetics and how you want your bathroom to make you feel, but evaluate the *layout* of the space too, and tailor your bathroom practically to your needs. A bathroom should be a sanctuary — a serene place in which you can literally wash away the troubles of the day — but it won't feel sanctuary-like if the layout means that you need to be Houdini to get into the bathtub without falling into the loo!

Of course, not everyone has the budget to remodel a bathroom, so making small changes — such as switching the fittings and fixtures, replacing bath panels and shower screens, or painting tiles — can be an affordable way to freshen up a bathroom and put your own stamp on it.

Make it Your Own

I talk a lot about flow throughout this book, in terms of colours and themes, but I love that we live in an era where we often see homes with a different aesthetic in every room. In the past there was a tendency to have very matchy-matchy rooms — for instance, the green bathroom suites of the 1970s, or the neutral looks seen in the 1990s, which would be mirrored, not only in all your bathrooms, but throughout your entire home. Now we are seeing homes that have a different style in every room, and I love that. You might want a vibrant and energizing maximalist living space, but after a long day at work you want to come home to calming boutique-hotel bathroom vibes with scented candles, fluffy robes and reclaimed stone.

The beauty is, there are no rules — it is your home and your sanctuary to curate as you please.

A stunning bathroom sanctuary — Carla Elliman (@carlaelliman)

Bathroom ◆ 173

Hand-painted tiles give this bathroom the wow factor
– Geri Sammut-Alessi (@overatno18)

Upgrade Your Tiles

Most bathrooms are heavy on the tile front, so if you have a home kitted out with tiles you don't love, that can really impact your enjoyment of the space. However, you can transform tiles far more easily than people think…and without ripping everything out! The two main options for a simple and easy refresh are to go over the tiles with peel-and-stick or to paint the existing ones. There are pros and cons to both.

Peel-and-stick

Pros

- Quick and easy to apply — this is a DIY that can be done in a couple of hours
- Affordable, you can buy a pack of ten tiles for a reasonable amount
- Easy to clean

Cons

- Some people find the adhesive doesn't last that well, though this can be remedied with the addition of spray adhesive
- Sometimes there is lifting of tiles in wetter areas and areas of high traffic
- Limited designs to choose from

Painted tiles

Pros

- You can create any design you like, and they will be entirely unique to you
- Affordable
- Easy to clean
- Durable

Cons

- The DIY can be a little more time consuming, if you are painting a design

As you can see, I'm team paint when it comes to a practical and affordable way to make over a bathroom. Don't be put off by the idea that painting tiles is any more tricky than other surfaces, with the right product, it is a simple and achieveable DIY with massive impact (for paint types, see pages 80–81).

How to Paint Tiles

You Will Need

Sugar soap

Primer (optional)

Tile paint

Stirrer

Roller tray

Foam or short-pile roller

Paint brush

Masking tape

Dust sheets

Protective glasses

Grout pen (optional, depending on the finish you would like)

Silicone sealer (optional)

1. **Prep:** Make sure to protect nearby areas with tape or dust sheets. And don't forget to protect you too, use glasses or googles to keep safe.

2. **Clean everything thoroughly:** For a professional finish, you need to make sure your tiles are well cleaned. Use sugar soap or degreaser to clean the area. Rinse off with water. Make sure tiles are completely dry before priming.

3. **Prime:** Some specialist tile paints have primer built in, so check your brand to see if you need to use a primer first. As tiles are a more difficult surface for paint to adhere to, it is important to check if you need to do this step. If you need to prime, use a roller to apply for an even finish. All primers are different, so follow the instructions on the tin.

   Some bathroom tile paints, such as Rust-oleum's range, come with an activation solution that needs to be added to the paint. If this is the case, be sure to follow the product guidance.

4. **The fun bit:** It's time to start seeing the change happen! Mix the paint well and then apply using a roller for a smooth finish. You might want to use a brush to get into the grout lines. Repeat for a second coat.

5. **Grout:** Depending on the look you want to achieve, once the paint dries you may want to go over the grout lines in a grout pen to achieve a defined finish. There are also grout paints available, I've even seen metallic colour options, for that ultimate dopamine hit!

6. **Seal:** Once the paint has dried, it's a good idea to apply silicone sealer over the paint where necessary. Particularly around any areas that get frequently wet, such as around the join between wall tiles and the sink.

7. **Wow factor:** Painting your tiles will make a huge difference, but why not go that extra step. I have seen lots of incredibly creative makeovers where spaces have been totally transformed through painting tiles, such as in the homes of Geri @overatno18 (see page 174) and Hannah @little_edwardian_semi, both of whom have created striking designs using tile stencils, or in Geri's case, a freehand design. It's a fantastic way to elevate your bathroom's appearance without the cost of replacing tiles.

Bathroom

Don't Rule Out Wallpaper!

One of the questions I'm asked most, is how my bathroom wallpaper is holding up. People have a hard time believing me when I say that it's not peeling off!

I love the impact of wallpaper, and it seems a shame that people are missing out on giving their bathrooms the wow factor they deserve. We've now had a wallpapered bathroom for over three years and, other than one corner slightly lifting, which is no more than any other wallpaper in our home, it's all still firmly adhered to the wall. If you are apprehensive, you can buy special wallpapers for bathrooms, and don't forget to apply a clear varnish to seal the wallpaper – it dries matte and clear, so makes no difference to the appearance.

My Top Wallpaper Tips

I've learned everything I know about wallpapering from my very patient other half, Jon, and am by no means an expert, but these are the essential tips that I have gathered on this part of my DIY journey. They are particularly relevant for patterned wallpapers.

1. **Measure, measure, MEASURE or repent at leisure.** I had no idea how important it is to make sure you use a plumb line and check if your walls are even. The last thing you want is to end up with a gap or wonky pattern, so put the prep in to check that your walls measure the same height along the length of the room. You will then be able to plan accordingly and leave an allowance when you hang your first drop. Of course, you can use a level to do the same job, but the plumb line is much cheaper!

2. **Always mark the top.** Label the top of the drop when you cut it. Yes, I have been known to stick it upside down in the past. Mark the top to avoid a meltdown.

3. **More is more.** When it comes to wallpaper paste: use lots. Having plenty of paste applied will mean that you can slide the paper around more freely, enabling you to match your pattern easily. This is especially true if it's a hot day as the glue dries quickly.

4. **Diagonal cuts are your friend.** For windows and doors, line up and paste the paper as usual, then find the frame of the window or door and make a diagonal cut in towards the frame. Now you can press into the shape and trim.

5. **Feel the fear.** I was reluctant to try wallpapering; I was scared that I would mess it up. But it's actually not that tricky, and there's nothing more satisfying than seeing a space come together that you have done yourself.

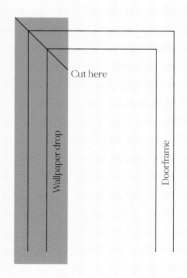

It's the Little Things

Not all changes you make in your home need to be huge ones; accessories, such as fun bathmats, cute colourful towels, art and plants, are all affordable ways to bring your bathroom to life. Surround yourself with decorative touches that make you smile, such as cheeky art and playful bathmats. And the best part is that you can switch them around as the mood takes you – a much quicker way to get a new look than redecorating.

Use Open Shelves

As in other areas of my home, I have chosen open shelves in our bathroom as the dual purpose of practical storage combined with the visual appeal makes them perfect for displaying my vases, art and plants. Beautiful baskets look good on bathroom shelves and can be employed to hide away any less aesthetically pleasing but essential bathroom bits, such as cleaning products and spare loo rolls.

Bye-bye Chrome

When we designed our bathroom, we had to navigate an endless sea of chrome to find our brass taps. Now there is much more choice available, and not just in brass but black and copper too, so you can really go all out. We used spray paint to transform some of the storage baskets and light fittings to achieve a coordinated golden glow throughout the space. Of course, if chrome floats your boat, then go with that, it's a classic for a reason!

Feel-good bathroom vibes offset by sleek black taps and accessories – Julie Choi (@letsby.avenue)

Bedrooms

Your bedroom is the one space above all others in your home where you want to feel relaxed.

Sleep is essential for good mental and physical health. Deep, restorative sleep allows our bodies to repair and restore – and studies have shown that creating the right sleep environment is a key component in ensuring you get the forty winks you need. Experts agree that the core elements of a great bedroom space are noise, light and temperature. So, choices on lighting and curtains or blinds will be crucial.

In our home we have an ongoing battle over the window dressings: I have a deep-seated love for romantic, pretty voiles. According to Jon, the only 'pretty' that they are is pretty useless. Like most, he prefers the blackest and darkest of black-out curtains to give that essential quality sleep. I'm at the stage of my life where I am so permanently exhausted by parenting and working that I can sleep anywhere and through anything (I am well known in my family for falling asleep in random spots all over the house), but should the moment come when I join the ranks of sensible people who shun voiles in the bedroom, I know I won't need to sacrifice much on the aesthetics front There are so many lovely curtains lined with black-out materials as well as all manner of beautiful printed blinds to block out those early rays and make sure you get the rest you need. Just don't tell Jon I said so! As well as ways to block light, you also want to make sure the lighting you have in your bedroom is soft and cocooning. No one wants to be shell shocked with stark white light when they first get up, and ambient, cosy light before bed is the perfect way to unwind. A combination of lamps as well as 'the big light' is always best, so that you can adjust the lighting to your mood.

Make it Your Own

Inevitably you will spend large parts of your time here resting and recharging, so you don't want this room to be somewhere that's either too clinical or overly stimulating. That doesn't mean you can't still stay true to your tastes — in our master bedroom, we have lent into my love of bold colours and created a sumptuous cocooning space. The dark blue-green ceiling counters the brighter turquoise walls, so that it still feels restful.

To reduce the chaos and clutter, all the bedrooms in our house have floor-to-ceiling wardrobes. This just makes sense for us as we have so much 'stuff'. The cupboards, which are mostly Ikea hacks, are painted to match the walls so that they blend in and help give the illusion of space in small rooms. Don't worry, it doesn't just have to be sensible choices: for instance, to make our wardrobes as charming as possible, we added decorative handles.

Remember: it's the little details that really pull a space together and make it perfectly yours.

Add a Fireplace for Design Warmth

I wanted to create a sense of escapism in our bedroom, which is why I added this faux fireplace. Yes, I almost certainly should have used the extra wall space for something sensible, like additional storage. However, when I'm lying in bed at night reading, I can glance up at the fireplace at the foot of the bed and almost convince myself I'm in *Downton Abbey*, a thing that makes me ridiculously happy. I'll never regret giving my boring old council house a bit of character and interest. The mirror above the fireplace also serves to reflect the light around the small room, as does the gold leaf inside it. So, although it's not functional in the sense of providing heat, it's working pretty hard as a decorative feature, and most importantly makes my heart sing when I see it first thing in the morning.

Soft Furnishings for Comfort and Style

In a space that is supposed to be restful and relaxing, sumptuous soft furnishings are key. These are also things that are quick to change-up in order to give your space a new look, especially if you like to change your decor with the seasons. A pretty, patterned bedspread will always lift my spirits, as will cosy throws and quirky cushions. There are loads of great and affordable bedding options, so consider what mood you would like to evoke and treat yourself to some fresh sheets or a throw to give your room a refresh.

How to Choose the Bed

The bed will be the most important piece of furniture you will buy for this room, but don't forget to consider the layout first. Our bedroom is fairly small, and Jon insisted on the biggest bed possible, so we now don't have any other option than to place the bed against the back wall. (In fairness, I'm blaming Jon but there was, of course, a spare wall where the fireplace now resides. Ahem, we'll just gloss over that!) Once you know where your bed will sit and what size bed that space dictates, you need to consider the style: you will want something that reflects your tastes, but also provides that sense of restfulness and comfort that you crave after a long day. I'm a sucker for a statement bed, but if you don't have one and are not in the market for a new one, they can be levelled up easily by making a homemade headboard or upcycling the one you have. Headboards can easily be covered, reupholstered, or even painted to give you a unique one-off piece.

Bedrooms • 187

How to Upholster a Headboard

Reupholstering sounds daunting and most of us wouldn't dream of attempting it. Of course, creating a beautiful bespoke armchair is probably best left to the professionals, but to reupholster a straight-edged headboard is probably not harder than most basic DIYs. Master the staple gun and you are halfway there!

You Will Need

Fabric scissors

Heavy staple gun (you might also need a staple remover, if your gun doesn't come with one)

Fabric of choice (make sure you choose something suitable; you will want a durable fabric, so think velvet rather than cotton or linen)

Padding (if using)

Tape measure

Fabric pins or tacks

Hammer

1. **Remove your headboard:** This will differ depending on the bed you have.

2. **Measure your headboard:** Use a tape measure to measure across the width and height.

3. **Cut the fabric to size:** Allow an extra 5cm (2in) each side to wrap.

4. **Cut padding to size:** If you are adding padding, cut this using the same measurements but without the additional 5cm (2in).

5. **Secure the fabric in place:** Make sure the material is snug but not so tight it puckers. Fabric pins or tacks are helpful for this stage.

6. **Staple gun:** Now it's time to bring the big guns out...by that I mean the staple gun! Start at the top centre and work your way around the underside of the headboard. When doing this be careful to make sure you are connecting with the frame, not just material or foam.

The Dopamine Home, Room by Room

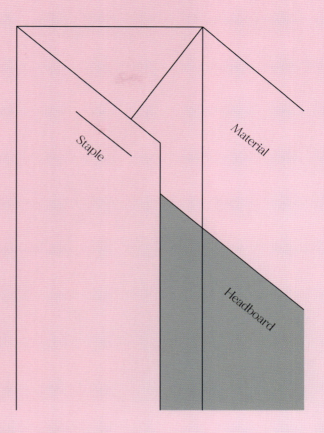

7. **Take care at the corners:** The corners are a little more work, you need to remove the excess fabric to avoid bunching to create a sharp edge. Do this by cutting a diagonal line into your fabric, fold the edges like you would wrap a nice gift and secure with the staple gun. Cut off any excess material.

8. **Reattach to the bed:** Refasten the headboard to the bed or wall.

Start Small

If this is your first attempt at upholstery you might want to practise first on something simple, such as a cushion pad.

Extra Storage

As well as our built-in cupboards we have bedside tables to provide extra storage. There are bedside storage solutions of all sizes available and, although mine are currently colour drenched the same shade as the walls, we have upcycled ones using wallpaper in the past, to make a fun feature.

    Under-bed storage can be a great option for stashing away clutter. After years of shoving everything under the bed, we went for an ottoman, and it's been a game changer. The fact it's velvet pink is a bonus, too.

    We also created some hidden storage when we built the stud wall to add our bedroom fireplace. What would have been dead space is instead a cupboard with a slim set of shelves where I store spare wallpaper and lots of toiletries. In a small house you need to make every corner work for you.

A painted ceiling instantly elevates a room — Hannah Clark (@little_edwardian_semi)

192 ◆ The Dopamine Home, Room by Room

Don't Forget the Ceiling!

People often forget the 'fifth wall' when it comes to painting their homes, but my deep-blue ceiling is one of my favourite feel-good features in our bedroom, it makes me feel incredibly cosy and relaxed. Critics might say that our rooms are too small for dark ceilings, but I disagree. There's nothing better than lying on your bed looking up into one of your favourite colours, rather than at an uninspired and forgotten white ceiling.

Top Tips to Create a Flawless Painted Ceiling

Remember: if you are decorating a whole room, paint the ceiling before the walls to avoid any downward splatters.

1. **Good prep is important.** So, say goodbye to cobwebs and sand any rough patches. Tape up any light fittings and put down dust sheets to catch drips. Use protective eyewear.

2. **Flat matte paint is your best choice,** unless you are purposely going for a sheen or shiny look.

3. **Cut in with a paint brush** round the perimeter first.

4. **Use a microfibre roller** on an extension pole for the main painting. It should be loaded with enough paint that you are able to roll on paint without applying pressure.

5. **Roll in the direction** of the main source of light (window) to minimize visible streaks.

6. **For each new roll,** start as far as possible into the previous section. It is important to always roll over a wet edge to avoid roller lines.

7. **Always apply a second coat.** Allow to dry fully then apply the second coat for a flawless finish.

Kids' Rooms

Decorating a kid's room is a wonderful opportunity to celebrate their unique personality and interests.

Children's bedrooms are one space in a home where you can really let your imagination and inner child run wild. In recent years, as our children have got older, decorating their rooms has become a collaborative process — we have worked together to come up with a design that harnesses their incredible imaginations, tempered with some parental practicality. Of course, including children in the process can open a can of worms, we had to talk our youngest out if a very red room recently! A good tip is to manage their expectations: flag up that the initial stage is brainstorming to get ideas, and that nothing is guaranteed, this will help avoid any disappointment from unrealistic expectations that you can afford everything on their wish list. We have really loved doing our children's rooms this way, and it's exciting and confidence-boosting for them to see how well their ideas come together, and to show we trust their input.

If your children are too young to help you with ideas, or simply not interested, and you are struggling, Pinterest and Instagram can provide endless inspiration. I have always looked to colourful, nature-based rooms for my children, as there is something that feels very pure and unspoiled about them.

Consider Changing Tastes

One thing to consider when incorporating your children's ideas is how quickly their passions change. My eldest is the perfect example of this, every Christmas his wish list will revolve entirely around one interest, only for him to have moved onto something completely new by the time he opens his presents! When decorating kids' rooms, try to keep the decor slightly more neutral with the theme running through the soft furnishing and accessories — these are much easier to switch out when their tastes evolve.

Shared rooms for siblings can be another tricky-to-navigate situation. Of course, you want to encourage each child's independence and for them to have their personality reflected in their decor, but you also want to create a cohesive space that is restful and harmonious. If your children want a space that is divided not only into zones but also into separate looks, then picking out accent colours to weave into both spaces, or the same pattern running throughout, will help keep the space unified.

A sweet shared space for siblings — Laura Hall (@thehexagonalhouse)

Keep it Restful

Just in the way that our room has combined our love of bold interiors with the need for Zen, similarly we have tried to balance playful and colourful in our children's rooms. Our son has always struggled with sleep, so a calmer palette suits him better and we have colour drenched the room in a soft green for a sense of peace. We have created a playful room with a rainbow mural painted on one wall, but this is behind the bed, and you only see it when you walk in rather than when you try to sleep, something to bear in mind if you are planning to add a feature wall and want to avoid feeling sensory overload before bedtime.

Kids' Rooms

Make it Multi-functional

We often need our children's bedrooms to fit many purposes; a restful sanctuary to sleep, a playroom, a space for creativity and, in some cases, a place to study. It can feel overwhelming to curate a room to meet all these needs but don't panic, with careful planning it is possible! The key is to make the space work hard, use every inch available to you. Floor space is important, especially for smaller children, so considering beds such a mid- or high-sleeper means that there is no wasted space. Having a taller bed isn't the only way to make the most of the height in a child's room, you can also go vertical with storage to keep toys off the ground, in nets or on hooks; display books on the walls; and style toys on shelves decoratively to bring the fun to functional!

The Snooze Factor

As a parent I have spent far too much time obsessing over my children's sleep, or lack of it, so making sure they have a comfy bed for deep slumber is something that benefits the whole household. But comfort isn't the only factor to consider when choosing a child's bed, the right bed can transform the room layout. I really don't think you can beat mid- or high-sleeper beds as they make such great space savers. And they aren't just practical – I have seen ones with slides, playhouses, desks and gaming stations incorporated! Other great options are trundle beds which have a pull-out for sleepovers – my boys are always asking for this option – or cabin beds with built-in storage. And don't forget, even if you have to err on the practical side, you can add lively bedding to inject some cheeriness.

Clever Storage

Considering their size, these small people come with a lot of 'stuff'. Toys, games, books and art equipment…it soon piles up, so you want to make sure you have adequate storage for all the trappings that come with kids. Using baskets to store toys in is a great idea as not only do they look great but are easily and safely accessible, and can be rotated to keep boredom at bay. Blanket boxes and ottomans, which provide seating as well as storage, are another great choice for multi-functional storage.

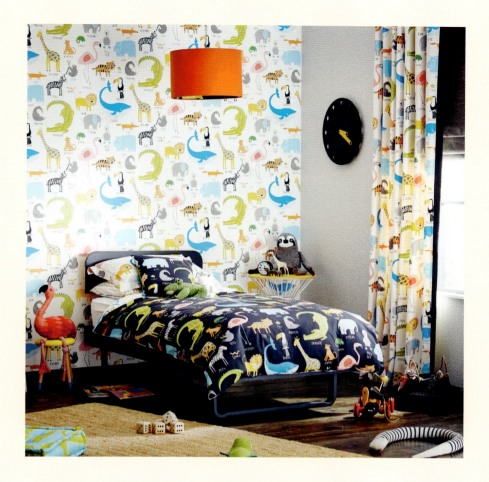

A Decorative Touch

As much as you can have fun decorating for children, you want to make sure that the resulting space has the right balance of a room that allows their imagination and creativity to flourish while not being so stimulating they are still bouncing around at bedtime. A way to do this is to make sure that their chosen theme doesn't overwhelm the space. If they love superheroes, put up that comic-strip wallpaper mural on one wall, but pair it with the rest of the walls painted in a less vivid tone. They want a jungle theme? You don't need to paint a full-blown rainforest replica, you can add jungle bedding, a few well-placed painted trees and add some fun animal toys. Taking a more measured approach to their brief also means that when they grow out of it (why does it happen so quickly?), it will be a far easier evolution.

Work definitely wouldn't feel a chore at this desk – Poppy Pearson (@letsgotopoppys)

Study or Workspace

Post-pandemic WFH has become the norm, with around a third of the population working from home at least some of the time.

While you might not have a dedicated study, many of you will have an area you work in, be it a corner in your bedroom, kitchen or dining room. These workspaces are places where we want to have high energy and be at our most productive, so it's important to curate a space that enables us to achieve this, while bearing in mind that it is often a multi-functional space. We don't want our beautiful, cosy living space compromised with harsh lights, papers everywhere, and the constant reminder of work, when we are in what is supposed to be a happy sanctuary. So, planning our workspaces carefully to ensure there are clear boundaries between home life and work life is key.

Design for Productivity

If you have a spare room that is mainly used as an office or a dedicated study, then decorating to include colours that promote energy — such as oranges, yellows and even some purple tones — is a great idea. You also want to make sure there is suitable lighting, possibly with the addition of a desk lamp. Ample storage is also essential. Remember that clutter can literally render us unable to think straight, which is not the ideal frame of mind for productive work. A tidy office with a place for everything is a guaranteed mood-boost when you sit down at your desk in the morning.

Making sure that you have a suitable desk and chair is a key to creating a comfortable, productive study space. Your desk and seat should, of course, be ergonomically suitable — no one will be brimming with creative ideas when they are hunched over the wrong-sized desk — but that doesn't mean you can't choose a work station that blends beautifully into your room, while also being conducive to work. For instance, if you are working in your bedroom you might want to find an attractive dressing table or writing desk that doesn't look out of place, and still has a beautiful bedroomy vibe. The last thing you want is an ugly obelisk spoiling your sanctuary.

No Monday blues in this light and creative space — Lou Crane (@notaperioddrama)

Study or Workspace

Get in the Zone

So, you may be working in your bedroom or the conservatory rather than that dream office, but that doesn't mean you have to let your work life and home life totally merge. Create 'zones' where you work. That could be by partitioning a space with pretty screens, using a rug as a marker or an alternative-coloured wall. Even down to simple changes, such as if you are using a dressing table that doubles as a desk, keep your work paraphernalia in a separate drawer to your usual bits and pieces to avoid the overlap between work and home.

WFH goals! – Poppy Pearson (@letsgotopoppys)

Take it Outside

Garden offices have become increasingly common with the rise of working from home, and for those with limited indoor space and some spare outdoor space, they are the ideal solution. With immaculate decor (I've even seen some with panelling), glazing, heating and Wi-Fi, these pimped-up sheds have evolved into something so sophisticated that I'd be tempted to move in there fully! Naturally, they are not all this fancy, and you can still create the perfect garden workspace on a smaller budget using a shed, an electric connection, and some well-styled office decor to assist productivity.

Garden

Since the pandemic, when, for a time, we were confined largely to our homes, there has been a rise in turning our outside spaces into multipurpose sanctuaries.

With the combination of gentle exercise, time spent outside and the need for quiet focus on the task at hand, gardening is a dopamine winner. And if you are less than green-fingered, I firmly believe that it's just as possible to achieve that same hit of happiness from relaxing in an outdoor space that you have designed.

Our outdoor spaces have never worked harder: we are no longer solely focused on growing our flowers, fresh salad and produce. We now want to harvest the tomatoes, prepare them in our outdoor kitchen, cook them in our alfresco pizza oven, then enjoy the feast surrounded by friends beneath the pergola!

Of course, we don't all have the luxury of a traditional back garden. Your space might look more like a balcony, yard, roof garden or a shared communal space. It's not so much the space that matters, but how you utilize it to bring you joy. If you only have limited space, make sure you prioritize the elements you will use most. If your passion is to grow flowers to fill your home with, then give a mini greenhouse the prime spot; if you love to work out, make sure there is clear space for your equipment; or if you're a lounge lizard who lives for catching rays, then plan your space around making a suntrap so relaxing you never want to leave.

Outdoor spaces can sometimes be an afterthought for those of us who aren't natural gardeners. However, with careful planning we can make these areas an extension of our homes and model them to meet our needs, while giving us that all- important fresh air and greenery that is so good for mind, body and soul.

A true garden oasis – Hayley Stuart (@iamhayleystuart)

Create a Chill-out Zone

Pergolas are a fantastic way to create a cosy chill-out area in your garden. Many have a cover to provide much-needed shelter from the elements, so you can enjoy your outdoor space all year round. They can be decorated with boho shades and lanterns, disco balls or trailing plants...the styling options are endless. Of course, not everyone can afford a full-size pergola, or has the space. A fun alternative is a mini pergola made of bamboo to fit your space, or a portable festoon light planter, which still enables you to create a zone with hanging lights.

Make Your Own Planter Pergola

This is a great way to get those pergola vibes on a smaller scale and create a little chill-out zone in your garden. You can add hanging festoon lights, disco balls and voile curtains, like we did, for some boho-holiday vibes.

You Will Need

4 large planters (all equal size, to fit your space. The larger they are, the sturdier the pergola will be, but you will need to bear your garden size in mind.)

Fence post mix

Plants (your chosen selection for the planters; herbs and scented plants are a great choice bringing an extra sensory element)

Compost (enough to fill planters)

8 thick bamboo canes (make sure they are long enough to achieve the height you desire)

Saw

Drill

Screw-bolts

Level

Voile curtains (optional)

Festoon lights (optional)

1. Drill holes in the top third of the planters for drainage. These will replace any drainage holes at the base, as these will be covered by concrete.

2. Use a saw to cut the bamboo to the desired height.

3. Place one bamboo cane into the centre of the first planter and add the concrete mix so that it fills two-thirds of the planter (follow packet instructions). This will harden very quickly, so you won't have to hold the bamboo in place for long. Repeat with other planters.

4. Place the planters into the square or rectangle shape you want them to be in.

5. Drill a hole towards the top of the four bamboo canes. Measure the distance from the top of the planter to the drill hole to make sure you get these roughly equal (it doesn't have to be perfect).

6. Next, attach the next four canes to create a square at the top of the pergola. Drill holes into each cane. If you want to add voile curtains, slide them onto the bamboo at this stage – before fixing in place.

   Use a level to make certain the connecting poles are straight, then attach with a screw through the corresponding drilled holes in the upright canes in the planters and bolt tightly.

7. Add soil and plants above the concrete line.

8. Hang festoon lights or other decorations, as desired.

9. Relax and enjoy!

Garden ◆ 211

Furnish Your Garden

There are so many fabulous garden sets available, from rattan sofas to retro deckchairs and colourful bistro sets. We are lucky enough to own several sets that we can station in different 'zones' in our garden. Our outdoor space is very much a work in progress as it was a dumping ground for our renovations for a long time. Our priority is creating somewhere gorgeous to socialize as our indoor space is limited, so having comfortable seating to entertain is essential. For us comfort is on a par with aesthetics, so we are always on the look for furniture that is vibrant and fun! But remember, as fabulous as the furniture looks in the warmer months, consider if you have anywhere to store it once the weather changes. Fortunately, we have an outhouse, but if you don't have that option there are covers that you can purchase to keep your outdoors furniture protected. Take it from me, chancing it and leaving them to the elements will mean paying out again.

Simple accessories can make your garden the perfect social space; while colourful garden furniture and clever design touches can bring the themes of your interior to your outdoors (opposite) – Poppy Pearson (@letsgotopoppys)

Add a Decorative Touch...Or Two!

You wouldn't dump a sofa in your lounge and call it a job well done, would you? To create a dreamy mood-boosting outside space, don't forget to apply all the design elements that you would to the interior of your home. Pay attention to the details: add patterned outdoor rugs, colourful cushions, charming lanterns and pretty parasols. Take it a step further by adding shelves to style an old fireplace or even a bath! In truth, the garden is a place where you can really let your imagination run wild, so make sure you give it the love and attention that it deserves.

Dining Out

From the pandemic-era pub shed to pizza oven stations and full-blown outdoor kitchens, we are making our gardens work harder than ever for us. I can absolutely see why, there aren't many better feelings than eating al fresco on holiday, so it makes sense we would try and emulate those feel-good vacation vibes at home. I don't have an outdoor kitchen, and possibly with my cooking skills it would be wasted on me, but I love the idea of gathering with friends and family and cooking and eating together, bougie BBQ vibes all year round.

Upgrade Your Patio

One really affordable way that we injected some character and colour into our garden was painting and stencilling our patio slabs. It has been one of the best decisions we have made, as it's given massive impact without the price tag of new flooring. The possibilities are endless too, as not only are there plenty of stencil designs out there, but you could also paint your own design freehand.

Perfectly painted patio and DIY outdoor kitchen = ultimate garden goals – Hayley Stuart (@iamhayleystuart)

Garden ● 215

Stencil Your Patio

Inspired by some of the incredible painted patios I has seen on Instagram over the years — in particular from Hayley Stuart (@iamhayleystuart) — I finally worked up the courage to attempt my own. I used masonry paint to create a bold contrasting pattern using a stencil from Dizzy Duck Designs. I was honestly so scared it would all flake off, but I couldn't be happier with how well it has held up.

You Will Need

- Masonry paint (Sandtex is brilliant for durability and Valspar have the best range of colours)
- Stencil (I used Dizzy Duck Designs (@dizzy_duck_designs). They create the stencil to the perfect size for your patio slab)
- Small, dense, foam paint roller
- Large paint roller on an extension pole
- Paint brush
- Masking tape
- Patio sealant (I used Everest block-paving sealant)

1. **Clean patio thoroughly:** This includes any weeding, then a thorough sweep and pressure wash.

2. **Watch the weather:** You need a day that is not too hot (or it may cause paint cracking), nor too cold. Wait until it is no cooler than 10°C at night — this is so important; the cold can cause paint peeling!

3. **Paint the base coat:** This is best done using a large roller on an extension pole. You usually need two coats. The drying time will depend on the paint; masonry paints typically take between one to four hours, but check your paint brand's guidance.

4. **Stencil!** Once the base coat is dry, you are ready to start stencilling. The key to getting crisp lines and no bleeding is to tape down the stencil in order to keep it tight to the paving slab. Use a small roller with a SMALL amount of paint. This will stop it seeping under and bleeding. Remove the stencil as soon as you have finished painting that slab. You can use a paint brush to touch up edges.

5. **Leave to cure:** In general, masonry paint can take several days to cure fully, or up to thirty days in some cases. For best results, you should follow the manufacturer's guidance.

6. **Seal:** Apply sealant over whole patio with a clean roller, once dry apply a second coat.

Acknowledgements

Never in my wildest dreams did I imagine I would be capable of writing a book, and that's what I would like you to take away with you once you finish reading this.

I want you to ignore those voices that tell you that you can't do something, or that it won't work out. So many people are afraid of DIY or decorating because they are worried about making mistakes. Well, so am I. But if we listen to that doubting inner critic, we will never try, and never learn and improve. If I, someone who is more comfortable writing a shopping list than a book, and who had never decorated a single home until a few years ago, is now a published author of an interior-design book, then you too can achieve things you didn't think possible.

Of course, having the courage and confidence to try new things has always been easier for me since I had Jon by my side – the best friend, partner and champion anyone could dream of. Grieving for a child can do terrible things to a relationship, but it brought us closer together. Ultimately, he was the only other person who truly knew how it felt to have lost Kit, and that forged our relationship in iron. Throughout all our ups and downs, he has been a constant and our rock. When I was poorly in hospital after my cancer surgery, he would come and wash my hair and tell me I would be OK when I no longer believed it. He has endless patience with all my projects, despite the house always being upside down. He has taught me everything I know and sorted out many a bodge job, as well as having countless ideas and always coming up with a solution when I am ready to give up. I don't know how I got so lucky.

Rudi and Arlo are just as patient as Jon with their rooms being upended for redecorating or dumping grounds for photoshoots. And when participating in Instagram content, they do it with minimal complaints...well, as long as a bribe is involved! More importantly, they are just an absolute joy and make us proud every day. We are also lucky to have such amazing support from wider friends and family, especially our parents who were the ones that made it possible for us to start this journey and who have held us up through the hardest of times.

The interiors community that I have met along the way on social media have also been a massive inspiration. Both personally, through the friendships I've made that will last a lifetime, and by way of their incredible dopamine interiors, many of which are featured in this book.

I hope that from reading this book, as well as taking away the confidence to try some dopamine DIY, you will realize there really are no rules and that creating a home that is unique to you and that fills you with a sense of happiness and pride is singularly the most important concept when it comes to decorating your home.

Also, big thanks to my lovely editor, Philippa Wilkinson, for her constant encouragement and help, as well as unfaltering energy and enthusiasm. Without her and the lovely Nicole Thomas and Andrew Roff, I would never have believed I could make this book a reality. And, of course, to Mietta Yans and Anna Stathaki for bringing it all together and making it look better than I could have hoped.

Rachel x

Resources

This book is filled with gorgeous imagery from my community of talented Instagram interior decorators, as well as some brilliant brands whose joy-inducing products epitomize the dopmaine trend. With special thanks to:

Brands:

Patch Plants

Houseplant experts and UK plant delivery service. Patch Plants' mission is to make gardening easy for everyone.

patchplants.com

Oliver Bonas

My go-to for dopamine-inducing home decor (plus fashion, gifts, jewellery and more!).

oliverbonas.com

Valspar

My go-to paint brand, they have an unrivalled colour range and brilliant product that never fails to deliver.

valsparpaint.co.uk

Scion Living

A British designed brand of colourful and playful pattern, with a Scandinavian influence.

scionliving.com

H&M Home

Affordable homewear at its best, H&M Home is the perfect place to look for a little something to lift your space.

hm.com

Lick

A paint brand with sustainability at its heart, Lick has a beautifully curated palette of colours as well as ingenious peel-and-stick samples.

lick.com

Influencers:

Carla Elliman, @carlaelliman

Charlotte Cannon, @homeofcharl

Ellie Lawrence, @sevenpalmtreehouse

Geri Sammut-Alessi, @overatno18

Glen Handley, @inside.number.twelve

Hayley Stuart, @iamhayleystuart

Hannah Clark, @little_edwardian_semi

Helen Ford, @homewithhelenandco

Janine Genower, @houseofedencourt

Joanne Hardcastle, @hardcastletowers

Julie Choi, @letsby.avenue

Laura Hall, @thehexagonalhouse

Laura Davies, @leopard_print_stairs

Lou Crane, @notaperioddrama

Nikki Shore, @weeny_victorian_house_in_ware

Poppy Pearson, @letsgotopoppys

Shona East, @honeyjoyhome

Sophia Ferrari Wills, @this colourfulnest

Steph Nicholson, @houseonthecorner_16

Picture Credits

The publishers would like to thank the following for supplying images:

p.2 Anna Stathaki; p.6 Anna Stathaki; p.15 Anna Stathaki; p.19 Anna Stathaki; p.20 Oliver Bonas, Dan Silby Art Direction/Styling and Carolyn Barber Photography. 2024; p.24 tl Janine Genower @houseofedencourt; p.24 tr Joanne Hardcastle @hardcastletowers; p.24 br Valspar; p.24 bl Laura Hall @thehexagonalhouse; p.27 Laura Hall @thehexagonalhouse; p.29 tl, bl and br all Helen Ford @homewithhelenandco; p.29 tr Poppy Pearson @letsgotopoppys; p.31 Followtheflow/Shutterstock; p.32 tl Nikki Shore @weeny_victorian_house_in_ware; p.32 tr Janine Genower @houseofedencourt; p.32 b Ground Picture/Shutterstock; p.34 Anna Stathaki; p.42 Valspar; p.47 Anna Stathaki; p.49 tl and br Steph @houseonthecorner_16; p.49 tr Pixel-Shot/Shutterstock; p.49 mr and bl H & M Hennes & Mauritz AB; p.50 tr and bl Pixel-Shot/Shutterstock; p.53 tl Janine Genower @houseofedencourt; p.53 r all H & M Hennes & Mauritz AB; p.53 bl Followtheflow/Shutterstock; p.54 tl, tr, br all Valspar; p.54 bl H & M Hennes & Mauritz AB; p.57 tl Lick; p.57 towel and jug H & M Hennes & Mauritz AB; p.57 tr Julie Choi @letsby.avenue; p.57 br Followtheflow/Shutterstock; p.57 ml Artem Avetisyan/Shutterstock; p.58 tl Shona East @honeyjoyhome; p.58 tr Julie Choi @letsby.avenue; p.58 mr Lick; p.58 b Ground Picture/Shutterstock; p.61 tl and br Valspar; p.61 tr Laura @leopard_print_stairs; p.61 bl Pixel-Shot/Shutterstock; p.61 ml Glen Handley @inside.number.twelve; p.62 tl and br Laura @ leopard_print_stairs; p.62 tr Carla Elliman @carlaelliman; p.62 bl Charlotte Cannon @homeofcharl; p.66 Anna Stathaki; p.69 Anna Stathaki; p.72 Charlotte Cannon @homeofcharl; p.77 Steph @houseonthecorner_16; p.80 bl Valpar; p.84 Oliver Bonas, Dan Silby Art Direction/Styling and Carolyn Barber Photography. 2024; p.87 Oliver Bonas, Dan Silby Art Direction/Styling and Carolyn Barber Photography. 2024; p.88 Sanderson Design Group, Scion; p.91 Sanderson Design Group, Scion; p.93 Sanderson Design Group, Scion; p.98-99 Patch Plants; p.100 Anna Stathaki; p.102 Anna Stathaki; p.105 Anna Stathaki; p.106 Followtheflow/Shutterstock ; p.109 l Charlotte Cannon @homeofcharl; p.111 tl, tr and br New Africa/Shutterstock; p.111 bl Pixel-Shot/Shutterstock; p.112 Anna Stathaki; p.118 Anna Stathaki; p.120 Anna Stathaki; p.123 Carla Elliman @carlaelliman; p.131 Oliver Bonas, Dan Silby Art Direction/Styling and Carolyn Barber Photography. 2024; p.133 FotoHelin/Shutterstock; p.134 Laura Hall @thehexagonalhouse; p.136 Carla Elliman @carlaelliman; p.139 Poppy Pearson @letsgotopoppys; p.140 Valspar; p.143 Helen Ford @homewithhelenandco; p.145 Anna St; p.147 Sophie Ferrari Wills @thiscolourfulnest; p.156 Valpar; p.157 Ellie @sevenpalmtreehouse; p.159 Joanne Hardcastle @hardcastletowers; p.160 Anna Stathaki; p.163 Helen Ford @homewithhelenandco; p.164 Hannah Clark @little_edwardian_semi; p.166 Charlotte Cannon @homeofcharl; p.169 Charlotte Cannon @homeofcharl; p.173 Carla Elliman @carlaelliman; p.174 Geri Sammut-Alessi @overatno18; p.177 stockwars/Shutterstock; p.181 Julie Choi @letsby.avenue; p.187 Anna Stathaki; p.192 Hannah Clark @little_edwardian_semi; p.196 bl Sanderson Design Group, Scion; p.197 Laura Hall @thehexagonalhouse; p.199 Sanderson Design Group, Scion; p.200 Poppy Pearson @letsgotopoppys; p.203 Lou Crane @notaperioddrama; p.204 Poppy Pearson @letsgotopoppys; p.205 Sanderson Design Group, Scion; p.208 Hayley Stuart @iamhayleystuart; p.212 Anna Stathaki; p.213 Poppy Pearson @letsgotopoppys; p.215 Hayley Stuart @iamhayleystuart; p.217 Anna Stathaki

Back cover image by Anna Stathaki

Index

DIY Index

Ceiling, Top Tips to Create a Flawless Painted 193

Cocktail Cabinet, Upcycle a 152–153

Gallery Wall, How to Curate and Hang a 128–130

Headboard, How to Upholster a 188–189

Painting Tips, My Top Five 82

Patio, Stencil Your 216–217

Pattern in Your Home, Five Easy Ways to Start With 92–93

Planter Pergola, Make Your Own 210–211

Radiator, Paint Your 132–133

Shelf-styling Tips, Simple 141

Stairs, My Top Three Tips for Painting 167

Tiles, How to Paint 176–177

Wallpaper, My Top Tips 179

Washing Machine, How to Paint Your 144

General Index

A
appliances 137 144
    colourful appliances 142
artworks 126
Atwood, Rebecca *Living with Colour* 52

B
bathrooms 171–81
    bathroom accessories 180
    bathroom fittings 181

bedrooms 183–93
    children 197–8
beds 86
    children's beds 198
    how to choose a bed 186
blues 56, 76
bold styles 25
Brooks, Gwendolyn 54

C
candles 109
ceilings 193
children 195–9
    changing tastes 196
chromotherapy 44
clutter 101
    clear outs 104
    everything in its place 103, 164
    living rooms 121
cocktail cabinets 155
    upcycle a cocktail cabinet 152–3
coffee corners 146
coffee tables 125
colour 43
    blues 56
    colour wheel 44–5
    eye-catching colours 64
    feel your way 46
    finding your colour style 64–5
    greens 55
    hallways 168
    kitchens 137
    neutrals 60
    orange and coral 51
    psychology of colour 44–6
    purples 59
    reds and pinks 48
    white 63
    yellows 52
    see palettes
concept boards 68
coral 51
curtains 86, 184–5

D
dining rooms 149–59
    get the dining table right 156
DIY 7–11, 38
    using leftovers 37–8
dopamine decor 8–11
    psychology of dopamine decor 17–19
    what is dopamine decor? 13–14
    what style do you like? 21–3

E
eclectic styles 26
eggshell paint 81

F
finding your colour style 64
    perils of social media 65
    practice makes perfect 65
fireplaces 122–3
    bedrooms 186
focal pieces 93
    coffee tables 125
functionality 151
    kid's rooms 198

G
gardens 207–17
    add a decorative touch 213
    garden furniture 212–13
    garden offices 205
gloss paint 80
greens 54, 55, 76

H
hallways 161–8
headboards 92, 186
home decorating 10–11
home offices 201–5
houseplants 96
    top five houseplants 98–9

K
Kandinsky, Wassily 46
Karen, Dawnn 13
kid's rooms 195–9
kitchens 135–46
    kitchen islands 147
Kondo, Marie 104
Kuo, Kathy 18

L
lighting 107
    bedrooms 184
    big light vs. little light 110
    get in the zone 108
    hallways 168
    making the most of dark corners 108
    mood lighting 109
living rooms 119–30

M
maximalism 14, 30
Meier, Richard 62
minimalism 30
moodboards 67–8

N
nature in your decor 95–9
    houseplants 96–9
neutrals 60
nostalgic styles 33

O
online buying 36
orange 51

P
painting 37–8, 79
    paint types 80–1
    to paint or not to paint? 83
palettes 71–2
pastel styles 25, 75
patios 214
    stencil your patio 216–17
patterns 89–90
    five easy ways to start with pattern 92–3

make it flow 91
pattern as a starting point 91
pergolas 209
    make your own planter pergola 210–11
pinks 48
planning 113–14
    be realistic about budget 115
    factor in time 115
primers 80, 82, 132, 144, 152, 176
purples 59

R
radiators 132–3
reds 48–9, 75
rugs 86, 87
    dining rooms 159
    patterns 93

S
satin paint 81
Scheib, Emma 104
seating 120
shelving 103
    bathrooms 181
    put on a display 139
    simple shelf-styling tips 141
shoestring decor 35
    fireplaces 123
    rugs 87
    tiles 90
    top five budget-friendly hacks 36
    unexpected red theory 49
Simon, Taylor Migliazzo 48
Smith, Joshua 17
sofas 86, 92, 105, 120, 125
    combining comfort and beauty 126
soft furnishings 86
    bedrooms 92, 186
specialist paints 81
stairs 167
storage 103–4

bedrooms 185, 190
dining rooms 155
hallways 162–4, 168
kid's rooms 198
storage checklist 105
studies 201–5
styles 21–3
    bold 25
    eclectic 26
    minimalism meets maximalism 30
    nostalgic 33
    pastel 29

T
textures 85–7
    soft furnishings that spark joy 86
    tactile elements for comfort 86
thriftiness 36
tiles 175
    stick-on tiles 90

U
unexpected red theory 48–9, 75
upcycling 38

V
Van Gogh, Vincent 53
vision boards 67

W
wallpaper 37, 90
    bathrooms 178
    top wallpaper tips 179
Watson-Smyth, Kate *Mad About the House* 130
white 62, 63
working from home 201
    creating a work zone 204
    design for productivity 202
    garden offices 205

Y
yellows 52

Index • 223

First published in Great Britain in 2025 by

Greenfinch
An imprint of Quercus Editions Ltd
Carmelite House
50 Victoria Embankment
London EC4Y 0DZ

An Hachette UK company
The authorised representative in the EEA is Hachette Ireland, 8 Castlecourt Centre, Dublin 15, D15 XTP3, Ireland (email: info@hbgi.ie)

Text copyright © 2025 Rachel Verney

The moral right of Rachel Verney to be identified as the author of this work has been asserted in accordance with the Copyright, Designs and Patents Act, 1988.

All rights reserved. No part of this publication may be reproduced or transmitted in any form or by any means, electronic or mechanical, including photocopy, recording, or any information storage and retrieval system, without permission in writing from the publisher.

A CIP catalogue record for this book is available from the British Library

HB ISBN 978-1-52944-189-5
Ebook ISBN 978-1-52944-190-1

Quercus Editions Ltd hereby exclude all liability to the extent permitted by law for any errors or omissions in this book and for any loss, damage or expense (whether direct or indirect) suffered by a third party relying on any information contained in this book.

10 9 8 7 6 5 4 3

Design by Mietta Yans

Printed and bound in Italy by L.E.G.O S.pA

Papers used by Greenfinch are from well-managed forests and other responsible sources